The

CURMUDGEON'S

GUIDE *to*

GETTING AHEAD

ALSO BY CHARLES MURRAY

Human Accomplishment

What It Means to Be a Libertarian

The Bell Curve

Losing Ground

Real Education

Coming Apart

The

CURMUDGEON'S

GUIDE *to*

GETTING AHEAD

DOS AND DON'TS OF RIGHT BEHAVIOR,
TOUGH THINKING, CLEAR WRITING,
AND LIVING A GOOD LIFE

CHARLES MURRAY

CROWN
BUSINESS
New York

Published in the United States by Crown Business, an imprint of
the Crown Publishing Group, a division of Random House LLC, a
Penguin Random House Company, New York.
www.crownpublishing.com

CROWN BUSINESS is a trademark and CROWN and the Rising Sun
colophon are registered trademarks of Random House LLC.

Crown Business books are available at special discounts for bulk
purchases for sales promotions or corporate use. Special editions,
including personalized covers, excerpts of existing books, or books
with corporate logos, can be created in large quantities for special
needs. For more information, contact Premium Sales at (212) 572-
2232 or e-mail specialmarkets@randomhouse.com.

Library of Congress Cataloging-in-Publication Data
Murray, Charles A.
   The curmudgeon's guide to getting ahead : dos and don'ts of right
behavior, tough thinking, clear writing, and living a good life /
Charles Murray.—First edition.
      pages cm
   1. Career development. 2. Success in business. 3. Business
communication. 4. Interpersonal communication. I. Title.
HF5381.M848 2014
650.1—dc23   2013045110

ISBN 978-0-8041-4144-4
eBook ISBN 978-0-8041-4145-1

Printed in the United States of America

10 9 8 7 6 5 4 3 2 1

First Edition

To Bennett,

Anna,

Sarawan,

and Narisara,

who have heard all of this repeatedly.

CONTENTS

ON THINKING AND WRITING WELL

55

ON THE FORMATION OF WHO YOU ARE

85

ON THE PURSUIT OF HAPPINESS

121

INTRODUCTION

The transition from college to adult life is treacherous. It is easy for new graduates to go directly to graduate studies that lock them into careers they will come to regret. Those who go directly to work are often in their first real jobs, not knowing how an office environment operates or how their supervisors are evaluating them. They often are emerging from universities that have ignored what used to be a central theme of university education: thinking about what it means to live a good life.

I wish I could tell you that this little book will fix all that. It won't, but it might help.

It began as a lark. My employer, the American Enterprise Institute (AEI), has an intranet site available only to its staff. About a year ago, some of my colleagues began running a series of tips for interns and entry-level staff on grammar and English usage. I decided to supplement it with a series of my own on proper behavior in the workplace. My wife and children have been calling me a curmudgeon for years because of my crotchety opinions. This was my chance to vent beyond the confines of the dinner table, but to such a small audience that I could give my unvarnished views without getting into trouble.

Over the next few months, I got enough encouragement from my readers that I expanded my topics first into tips about writing and then into more cosmic topics about life in general. Eventually I decided that I could broaden the audience without getting into *too* much trouble, and assembled the series into the book that you hold in your hand.

I wrote these tips with some assumptions about you, my reader:

You are in or near your twenties. You are intelligent. It's not essential that you have a college degree, but you probably do. Many of you attended a well-known college or university; some of you attended an elite one. You are ambitious—you daydream about becoming a CEO, a high-powered lawyer, head of the World Bank, Pulitzer Prize winner, or president of the United States.

Your ambitions are not confined to outward measures of success. You want to become excellent at something. You plan to marry eventually, if you have not already. You aspire to be a good person. You aspire to genuine happiness.

To put it another way, you are me long ago. For better or worse, I am giving you the same advice I would give to that vanished person.

As *The Curmudgeon's Guide to Getting Ahead* moves from success in the workplace into the deeper waters of success in living, you will find the occasional bromide, because some of the clichés you've been hearing all your life are actually true and need to be considered afresh. But I hope that most of the tips will offer ideas and options that you have not considered.

Charles Murray
Burkittsville, Maryland
November 26, 2013

ON THE PRESENTATION OF SELF
IN THE WORKPLACE

The first thing you need to understand is that most large organizations in the private sector are run by curmudgeons like me. That statement may not be true of organizations in the entertainment or information technology (IT) industries, which are often filled with senior executives who are either young themselves or trying to be. But it is true of most large for-profit businesses, nonprofits, foundations, law firms, and financial institutions. Academia goes both ways, with many professors who try to be best buddies with their students but a few who are world-class curmudgeons.

Technically, a curmudgeon is an ill-tempered old man. I use the term more broadly to describe highly successful people of both genders who are inwardly grumpy about many aspects of contemporary culture, make quick and pitiless judgments about your behavior in the workplace, and don't hesitate to act on those judgments in deciding who gets promoted and who gets fired.

Be warned that curmudgeons usually don't give off many clues that they're doing these things. I'm an example. I don't snap at subordinates. When someone approaches me, I like to think that I'm accessible and friendly. I try to express any criticisms cheerfully and tactfully. And yet behind my civilized public persona I am perpetually ticking off things in my head about the employees I encounter, both pluses and minuses, filing them away, and when the time comes for performance reviews, those judgments shape my responses.

Lots of the senior people in your workplace who can help or hinder your career are closeted curmudgeons like me, including executives in their forties who have every appearance of being open minded and cool. By their fifties, the probability that they are curmudgeons has risen precipitously. By their sixties, you can just about bank on it, no matter how benign their public presentation of self may be.

Curmudgeons of all ages and both genders remain closeted partly because they want to be polite, but also because they don't want to sound like geezers, old and out of touch. Voicing curmudgeonly opinions would instantly label them as such. So they never admit that they judge you on the basis of their inner curmudgeon—

but they do. If you want to get ahead, you should avoid doing things that will make them write you off.

These tips about how to behave in the workplace range from matters of style to the meat of your work. Some of them advise you to conform to your curmudgeons' prejudices on matters that you may think should be no one's business but your own. But let's get one thing straight at the outset:

1. Don't suck up.

Let's assume that you're going to work for a quality organization in the private sector. Within that organization, some of the people who run the place will be extremely good at what they do, some will be merely competent, and some will conform to the Peter Principle ("Employees tend to rise to their level of incompetence"). It's not a good idea to suck up to any of them.

By *sucking up*, I mean flattering supervisors, pretending to agree with their bad ideas, or otherwise unctuously trying to ingratiate yourself with them. Sucking up is usually thought to be a great way to get ahead, so this advice requires some explanation.

My career has brought me into contact with many highly successful people from the corporate, financial, publishing, journalistic, and scholarly worlds. Maybe I've just been lucky, but I have to go by my experience: Just about all of the highly successful people I've dealt with have been impressively skilled. I cannot think of any who got to their prominent positions by faking it. They have also almost always been self-confident, not in need of stroking, and good judges of people.

Caveat

I have had no experience with highly successful people in the entertainment industry or in government bureaucracies, where my advice may not apply. In politics, sucking up is part of the job description.

If the highly successful people in your organization are like that, trying to tell them they're wonderful will be a disaster. They will recognize what you're doing and disdain you for it. And it's not going to work much better with other supervisors. You don't want to suck up to the less competent or the incompetent, because (1) they probably are not in a position to help you much anyway, and (2) there's too much danger that the people you really want to impress will observe your sycophancy and remember it.

The flip side is that highly successful people tend to value honesty and courage. I'm not recommending that you go out of your way to disagree with them or otherwise show your independence. It's appropriate to be tactful if you're a junior person working with a senior person, and you certainly don't want to be abrasive. Just don't trim your views if they go against the grain of the discussion. Express yourself forthrightly, and the odds are that you'll get points for it.

If I'm wrong, and you find yourself in an organization where sucking up is in fact a good way to get ahead, look for a new job. It's not a quality organization after all, no matter how glittering its public reputation may be. Life is too short to work there.

2. Don't use first names with people considerably older than you until asked, and sometimes not even then.

I have in my library the three-volume collected correspondence, stretching over a half century, between James Madison and Thomas Jefferson. Their friendship was deep and intimate. And yet the last letter from Jefferson to Madison, written less than a month before Jefferson's death, begins not with "Dear Jemmy" (Madison's nickname), but with "Dear Sir." It concludes "most affectionately yours, Th. Jefferson." Not "Tom" or "Thomas," but "Th. Jefferson."

Ah, for the good old days.

The use of first names has undergone a cultural transformation in the last three or four decades, so that by now the use of honorifics and last names is nearly extinct. It's not just the telemarketer on the other end of the phone who calls you by your first name. I have had parents introduce me to their six-year-old with the words "This is Charles," requiring me to choke back an overwhelming urge to pat the little one on the head and say, "But you may call me Sir."

I blame this misbegotten use of first names on the baby boomers. Frightened of being grown-ups since they were in college, they have shied from anything that reminds them they're not kids anymore. But we're not talking about your social interactions with random aging boomers. We're talking about your professional interactions with highly successful older people whose good opinions you would like to acquire. By and large, highly successful people are quite aware that they are grown-ups. So cater to them: Call them by their last names until invited to do otherwise.

Often the invitation will be offered the first time you meet that highly successful person—"Call me Bill," says Mr. Smith. But before you respond with "Sure, Bill," consider what's going on.

One possibility is that Bill is serious, in which case "Sure, Bill" does you no harm. But another possibility is that Bill is going through the motions because he doesn't want to appear old and grumpy. In that case, suppose you thank him without using "Bill" and subsequently, unobtrusively, continue to refer to him as Mr. Smith. It's a no-lose proposition. If Mr. Smith really likes being called Bill by new employees forty years his junior, it will give him a chance to say so and show what a nice guy he is. If Bill is a closeted curmudgeon, his opinion of you will rise.

Another consideration is this: If you start out your relationship with a highly successful older person on a "Mr." or "Ms." basis, you can look forward to a satisfying moment down the road: At some point, when you have proved yourself, Mr. Smith is going to say to you, "I think it's time you called me Bill." The pleasure of that moment is inestimable.

3. Excise the word *like* from your spoken English.

Do you use the word *like* as a verbal tic? I mean, like, do you insert it in, like, random points in your, like, spoken conversation? If the answer is yes, this is the single most important tip in the entire book:

STOP IT.

I cannot think of another flaw among members of recent generations (this has been going on since at least the 1990s) that irritates curmudgeons more. Many of us have a hard time staying in a conversation with people who use *like* in every sentence. We resist hiring them. If assigned such people on our staffs, we avoid interacting with them. Yes, our reactions really can be that extreme. Even moderate use of *like* as a verbal tic lowers our estimate of the offender's IQ and moral worth.

How many of the people who can help or hinder your career feel as strongly about the *like* tic as I do? More than you might think. I am struck by the high percentage of people who have risen to senior positions who also care deeply about the proper use of the English language. That kind of pickiness is common not just in professions like mine, where the English language is our stock-in-trade. A surprising number of senior executives in corporations that make soap or machine tools are picky about good English. An even higher proportion of them are obsessively precise about everything. To people who love the English language and are precise, your use of *like* as a verbal tic is a proclamation that you don't love the language and are sloppy. Unfair? Maybe. But that won't keep us from writing you off.

4. Stop "reaching out" and "sharing," and other prohibitions.

In every era, novel ways of saying something get picked up, and soon thereafter what was once evocative becomes stale. I start with the Big Three—*share, reach out,* and *be there for you*—that unequivocally should be struck from your spoken and written language, then proceed to somewhat less offensive fads. The final ones are overused by just about everybody in Washington, where I work. I'm not sure how much of a problem they are elsewhere. But you can extrapolate from these examples to trendy phrases that are used in your industry and put yourself on guard against them.

Share. People don't just *tell* people things anymore. They *share* them. I suppose this fad got started because it conveys an attractive sense of bringing the other person into your personal circle. And sometimes *share* is the correct word. If your coworker has just explained his weird behavior by revealing that he has Tourette's syndrome, that's pretty personal, and it's okay for you to respond with "Thanks for sharing." But if your coworker tells you that he will be tied up in a meeting for the next hour, the simple "Thanks for telling me" is correct, and "Thanks for sharing" is sappy.

Reach out. If I sense that my coworker is troubled and so I take him out for a drink after work to give him a chance to confide, I'm reaching out to him. If I just want some company, I'm not reaching out. I'm inviting him to have a drink with me. *Reach out* is not the same as *invite* or *inquire*. Use the right word.

Be there for you. "I'll be there for you" has come to mean "I hereby make a meaningless pretend commitment." It's not going to make your friend feel better. If you are serious, be more specific, as in, "Who do you want me to kill?" or—revolutionary idea—*actually* being there for your friend, as in saying "Sounds to me like you could use some company. I'll be there in ten minutes." Similarly, thanking someone by saying, "Joe has always been there for me" is a wishy-washy way of conveying appreciation. Joe will feel a lot more gratified if you are specific and emphatic.

Impact used as a verb. The use of *impact* as a verb, when what you mean is *affect*, has gotten out of hand. The correct meaning of *impact* as a verb is to come into forcible contact with another object. A collision is involved. The next time you hear someone say that something "impacted" something, ask yourself if the imagery of one object colliding with another is appropriate. The answer will almost invariably be no. When choosing a verb, be content with *affect* and save *impact* for when you intend the imagery that the word is supposed to convey.

Interface. It means the same thing as *interact*, except that it is appropriately used to describe connections between machines, not human beings. When you stop to think about it, *interface* is also a strikingly cold substitution for *interact* when human beings are involved.

Issues. You can have issues with your spouse about your political views, but not about your infidelities. In the latter case, you don't have a position to defend. You can't have issues with alcohol or bipolar disorder. They aren't arguing back. Stop using *issues* as a euphemism for *a problem.*

Brand, as in brand yourself or branding, referring to human beings. Start by recalling what *branding* originally meant: a trademark burned into a product—or, in the case of animals, burned into the flesh. Why would you aspire to be labeled and defined so that your subsequent behavior must conform to the "brand" that you have established?

Data mispronounced and used as a singular noun. This is not a fad, but it's important to me and so I'll include it here. People who deal with data professionally know that the first syllable of *data* rhymes with "rate," not "rat." The word is plural, so they say "The data reveal that . . . ," not "The data reveals that . . . ." You will hear some prominent people, especially television journalists, pronounce *data* incorrectly. I am told that the style manuals at some major publications now say that it's permissible to treat *data* as singular. Do not lower yourself to their level.

Going forward. This is an example of a phrase that sounds good the first time you hear it used in its new meaning of "next," or "in the future," or "from now on" (e.g., "This will be our strategy going forward"). But after you hear it repeatedly, it grates. Just say, "This will be our strategy from now on." It's cleaner.

Grow, referring to something that is not a plant or some other living thing, as in "grow your business" or "grow the economy." It is a corruption of a perfectly good verb for no reason. The English language has plenty of ways to talk about expanding or enhancing nonliving things.

Drill down. The first time I heard *drill down,* I thought it was an effective image—going deeper into a complex issue. Many other people had the same reaction and so we all started using it. Now it is a cliché.

Incentivize. What's wrong with just saying that you want to "create incentives"? Besides being overused, *incentivize* has an ugly connotation of manipulating people to do things, while the noun *incentive* evokes people determining that something is in their self-interest and acting upon that judgment—a more respectful image.

At the end of the day. This was originally an evocative way of referring to the eventual result after a prolonged negotiation or political debate (e.g., "At the end of the day, the Democrats will have to settle for X and the Republicans will have to yield on Y.") As in the case of *drill down*, overuse has destroyed its initial charm.

By now you get the idea. For similar reasons, avoid using *dialog*, *liaise*, or *prioritize* as verbs. Avoid politically correct monstrosities such as *differently abled*. Avoid *proactive*, *paradigm*, *stakeholder*, and *point in time*. Avoid the trite, pretentious, jargony, or any word or phrase that reminds you of the way bureaucrats talk.

5. On the proper use of strong language.

One of the things that curmudgeons have a hard time believing about the twenty-something generation is that the *f*-word in all its variants has become for many of them just another word, not much more intense than *darn* was for my generation. But people who are in a position to know have persuaded me that it has become just another mild expletive among a good many Millennials.

Even so, my advice is that you never use it around senior executives unless you know for a fact that they use it freely themselves. A friend of mine who runs a large business was recently told that an applicant for an entry-level position had used the *f*-word twice in the job interview. The applicant didn't get the job. But my friend vehemently expressed his regret that he hadn't personally been present to terminate the interview the moment the word first came out of the applicant's mouth. You aren't going to get any points for using it, and you might get the death sentence.

I'm told that none of this advice applies if you work in the entertainment or IT industries, where the use of the *f*-word is as obligatory as the use of *like*. I don't know from personal experience. I'd still be cautious at the outset.

It's not that curmudgeons don't use the *f*-word. Some don't—a surprising number of highly successful people don't swear at all—but most of us (including me) do. But we try to use strong language appropriately, and that's the point of the rest of this tip.

Life's vagaries confront us with situations that call for us to express the full range of reactions. One of the glories of the English language is that it has vocabulary that can be called upon for all those situations. The heedless younger generation has frittered away that patrimony. Explain it to me: If you use the *f*-word as a kind of oral punctuation mark, how do you convey to your fellow human beings that you are really, truly shocked or angry about something? Say it five times in a row? The dialogue on some cable TV shows suggests that is indeed today's solution. It's pathetic.

What's true of the *f*-word is also true of the other

classic Anglo-Saxon monosyllables. Their ubiquitous use is tiresome and pointless, casts a thin coat of grime over the conversational landscape, and degrades your ability to draw upon their shock value when needed.

Consider your own need to get your point across when you're dealing with coworkers. Here's some advice for doing so. We all unconsciously calibrate where the people we know fall on the strong language continuum. Some people (e.g., many of your mothers) can get our immediate attention if they use even *damn*, because we know that *damn* for them is the equivalent of a barrage of obscenities from someone else. If you become such a person to those around you, advantages accrue.

First, abstaining from casual obscenity gives you the aura of an adult. Maybe I'm just out of touch, but ask yourself if I might be right: No matter how commonly the classic Anglo-Saxon monosyllables are used, they continue to carry with them a whiff of the jejune. In some small way, they say to those around you, "See, I'm still not a grown-up." That's not something you really want to advertise in a job setting.

Second, abstaining from casual obscenity lets you be precise about distinguishing among the times when you are mildly critical, seriously displeased, and outright angry, without appearing out of control or flummoxed. Go back to my earlier point: If using even *damn* is unusual for you, you can let a colleague or subordinate know that you are irked simply by sticking *damn* into an otherwise unremarkable instruction, delivered in an even tone of voice. If that's the case, imagine how easy it is to scare the living daylights out of them just by ratcheting your interjection another level or two up the vulgarity ladder.

Third, it is a lot of fun, once you have established a restrained persona, to watch the startled look on others' faces when you do let loose. You will instantly have their complete and perhaps terrified attention.

6. On piercings, tattoos, and hair of a color not known to nature.

If you have visible tattoos, piercings, or hair of a color not found in nature, curmudgeons will not hire you except for positions where they don't have to see you, and perhaps not even those. If you are hired by someone else, curmudgeons will not give you a fair chance to prove yourself. In such cases, we judge on appearances, thinking that you embody that which we find most distasteful about the current cultural sensibility.

I know that it's terribly unfair. But you won't get anywhere by trying to reason with us. For example, don't point out to us that women have pierced their ears for millennia. Yes, we will respond, women have pierced their ears—to more attractively adorn themselves with earrings. Curmudgeons understand that almost any earring is more attractive, not to mention more comfortable, if it is not clipped to the earlobe. Earlobe piercing is a means to an aesthetic end, not an end in itself. There is no way (in our view) to argue that a pin through an eyebrow is anything but disfigurement.

What About Earrings on Males?

Male curmudgeons think that men aren't supposed to be adorned (I'm not sure what female curmudgeons think). So no earrings, guys. Keep the watches utilitarian. Understated cuff links, if any. No rings except wedding bands. Nothing that sparkles.

As for tattoos, it does no good to remind curmudgeons that tattoos have also been around for millennia. Yes, we will agree, tattoos have been common—first among savage tribes and then, more recently, among the lowest classes of Western societies. In America, tattoos have until the last few decades been the unambiguous badge of the proletariat or worse—an association still acknowledged in the phrase *tramp stamp*. And don't try to tell curmudgeons that tattoos have become an art form. In the first place, we think that's like trying to say that paintings of Elvis on dinner plates are an art form. In the second place, any time a curmudgeon sees a tattoo, he is thinking about how it will look when its bearer turns sixty. Curmudgeons will cut you some slack if you are a former member of the armed forces with a well-executed tattoo of your unit's insignia. Otherwise, show up with a visible tattoo and you are toast before you open your mouth.

I personally am not as hard-core about hair. Purple, orange, green, or fire-engine-red hair is not as completely disqualifying to me as piercings or tattoos. Other curmudgeons may feel more strongly. But it's the difference between starting out with only two strikes against you as opposed to three. Why make life tough on yourself?

7. Negotiating the minefield of contemporary office dress.

Some of you work for organizations that have a clearly understood dress code. If that's the case, you may skip this tip. But many organizations haven't spelled out a dress code and you as a new employee are in the dark.

In the old days, it was simple. Certain kinds of attire were suitable for office wear, everyone had a good idea what that meant, and the senior people in the office were openly affronted when someone violated the unwritten code. A few decades ago, I had dashed into the office just to pick up something and leave. I wasn't going to be in the building more than ten minutes, so I arrived wearing a flannel shirt and jeans. As I was standing in front of the tenth-floor elevators waiting to leave, one of those elevators opened and out stepped Irving Kristol, AEI's most revered scholar. Irving was a warm and unpretentious person and a good friend. But there was no warmth in his eyes as he deliberately looked me up and down; said, "Well, what have we here?"; and walked away without another word. From that day until his death, long after it had become customary for AEI scholars to work in shirtsleeves, I never arrived at AEI in anything except a coat and tie.

Even twenty years ago, that kind of reprimand was becoming rare. By now, it is almost nonexistent. Senior people have gotten timid about enforcing unwritten rules, and that makes their well-meaning hypocrisy treacherous for twenty-somethings. In an age of sexual harassment complaints, it is objectively foolhardy for a male supervisor to comment on a female employee's dress, but the reluctance runs deeper than that, and it affects both male and female supervisors. "Suitable" and "unsuitable" office attire have become nebulous concepts; consequently, criticizing an employee's dress now feels queasily personal. But that's where the hypocrisy comes in. Most curmudgeons are unwilling to say anything to you, but the way you dress can nonetheless make them decide you are a nonserious person and lose interest in you.

Do not take your cue from the way your peers dress. They may be oblivious to the subtleties of an unwritten dress code. Until you are sure you understand what the expectations are, follow the lead of senior people of your gender regarding dress, and supplement those choices with good grooming: hair not still straggly damp from the shower, shirttail tucked in, underwear hidden— that sort of thing. And always be aware that what passes for good grooming and fashion among people in their twenties can still make you look like a slob to people in their fifties.

8. Office emails are not texts to friends.

Proper email and text etiquette is still evolving, and the last people you should ask for advice are people my age. David Shipley and Will Schwalbe coauthored a book on proper emailing practices titled *Send* that I recommend as a sort of *Fowler's* for cyberspace.

But emails to curmudgeons are a special case. Curmudgeons grew up with memoranda and snail-mail correspondence, and old habits die hard. A few simple precautions will keep you safe from disapproval.

For salutations, start formal and work down. If it's your first email exchange, you can't go wrong with using "Dear _____." If the response comes back "Hi _____," feel free to use "Hi" from then on.

While I'm on the subject of salutations, should there be any salutation at all? FWIW, here are my own guidelines: If my correspondent is a close associate with whom I exchange emails almost daily, I usually omit a salutation and don't expect a salutation in reply. If I am emailing someone less close and the email is the first in an exchange, I use a salutation—generally "Hi _____," unless I sense that my correspondent might prefer "Dear _____" (for example, because I know the person is old like me). I omit a salutation in subsequent emails that follow closely upon one another.

Some acronyms are okay, but cute spelling abbreviations aren't. Some curmudgeons use acronyms (see FWIW above), and you should feel free to respond in kind. But be careful—curmudgeons tend to think they are up to speed when they really aren't, and you can easily throw in an acronym that baffles them. Spelling abbreviations are another matter; even young employees have told me they are put off by "u," "ur," "4," and the like. So eschew spelling abbreviations that aren't Latin (e.g., "e.g." is okay).

Correct syntax and punctuation. When texting friends on my smart phone, I am likely to omit an apostrophe rather than going through the extra clicks necessary to insert it, and I am often casual about syntax. Office emails written on a computer call for a higher standard. For emails that are more than a few lines long, follow two simple routines: (1) Ask yourself if you would use the same syntax and punctuation if the email were being typed and you had to put your signature on it, and (2) *always* proofread your email before you hit "send." Spell check is helpful but not foolproof, and grammar checkers are even more fallible.

Acknowledge receipt. Things get lost in cyberspace. Emails scroll off the screen and are forgotten. So if you get an email that contains an instruction or a notification, make sure you let the sender know right away that you got it. My standard response in such cases is a one-word reply, "Roger." When someone complies with a request and sends me an email informing me, I reply with a one-word "Thanks!" to let them know I got it.

9. What to do if you have a bad boss.

Let's reverse the usual topic of these tips—how your supervisor is assessing you—and assess whether you should put up with your boss. You've been working at your new job for six months, let's say, and you're so unhappy with your supervisor that you're considering quitting. Here's what you need to think through: Exactly what is bothering you?

There is one immediate deal-breaker: The boss asks you to do things that you believe to be unethical or otherwise morally wrong. In that case, you should be prepared to quit. Before you actually take that step, however, go to some other senior person in the organization whom you respect and tell that person your story. If the result satisfies you, fine. If effective action isn't taken, quit. When you're in your twenties and you don't have a family to support, there's no reason to compromise your integrity to keep a job.

The Perfect Solution to the *He or She* Problem

I just used *he* in the preceding paragraph instead of *he or she*, and I will continue to do so throughout the rest of the book. Here's why:

The feminist revolution has tied writers into knots when it comes to the third-person singular pronoun. Using the masculine pronoun as the default has been proscribed. Some male writers get around this problem by defaulting to the feminine singular pronoun, which I think is icky. Using the gender-neutral *they* and *them* as substitutes for the singular pronoun is becoming common, and I can accept this jury-rigged solution for spoken English, but I hate to use it for written text. For a quarter of a century now, I have been promoting this solution: Unless there is an obvious reason not to, use the gender of the author or, in a cowritten text, the gender of the principal author.

It's the perfect solution. Whether we're talking about books, articles, office memos, or emails, just about as many women as men are writing them these days. If we all adopt my solution, there will be no gender pronoun imbalance in the sum total of English text. And all of us will be freed from the clunkiness of *he or she*, not to mention the barbarity of *s/he*. What's not to like?

What about a boss who is a nice person but incompetent? The incompetence might take many forms. Perhaps your boss is a lousy manager, giving contradictory instructions, failing to check whether his instructions have been carried out and unable to meet deadlines. Perhaps he makes factual or computational errors in the products he turns out. Perhaps he misunderstands the instructions given to him from above and sends you off on a task that you know his supervisors didn't have in mind. Whatever the specifics, it's quite clear: Your boss doesn't know what he's doing.

You have to ask how much his incompetence is holding you back. If you are trying to acquire a specific skill set, the answer may be "a lot." If you want to improve your craft as an editor in a publishing house, for example, it is important that you work under someone who is a terrific editor. The less specific the skill set, the more likely that you aren't losing much because of the boss's incompetence. You can learn a lot about good management by working under someone who is a bad manager. Sometimes incompetent people delegate so much work to their subordinates that you find yourself given meatier tasks than you would get from a more competent supervisor. Unless you need a boss from whom you can learn specific technical skills, you might as well stay on the job, though you might want to quietly test your alternatives in the local job market.

What about the boss who is a jerk? It depends on what kind of jerk he is. Let's start with the most notorious kind of office jerk, the sexist male who makes life miserable for his female colleagues or subordinates. I don't want to minimize how trying and even frightening it can be to deal with such a situation if you are a young woman new to the workplace and the jerk is a much older senior employee. But if you find yourself in such a situation, remember two things. First, even the hint of a formal sexual harassment complaint scares employers, who badly want to avoid the legal hassle and the financial costs that a complaint entails, and should scare the sexist jerk even more—his job can easily be in jeopardy. Second, you shouldn't assume you have to do battle all by yourself. Every office I've ever worked in has had sagacious women who would have been wonderful counselors and advocates for a young female employee who is being harassed. And let me put in a word for male curmudgeons. Most of us see ourselves as gentlemen. You don't have to approve of our antediluvian mind-set, but there's something to be said for having a senior male in authority who detests men who maltreat women or take advantage of underlings. You can come talk to us too.

The same generic advice applies if you are black and have a racist boss or you are gay and have a homophobic boss. You have legal options for responding, but they aren't your only options. Don't underestimate the decency of the other people in your workplace, including the curmudgeons.

Next we come to jerks who are merely unpleasant.

They are crude, controlling, ill-tempered, or otherwise offensive. How you react depends on how good they are professionally. When they are very good at doing something that you want to become good at, I'd stay on the job. The best of all possible ways to improve your professional skills is to be around such a person. The woman who inspired *The Devil Wears Prada* might have been a terrific pain to work for, but she apparently knew her stuff better than just about anybody in her business, and working as her assistant was probably an invaluable experience. The less spectacularly talented your boss is, the less reason you have to stay.

But in all cases when you have problems in your interactions with your boss, there's one more question you have to ask yourself: To what extent is your boss at fault, and to what extent are you a neophyte about supervisor-subordinate relationships? Some of you have reached your twenties without ever having been treated as a subordinate and you are not used to it. What you see as arbitrary, insensitive, or hostile behavior on the part of your boss may be nothing more than the way in which supervisors have been treating subordinates from time immemorial. People in charge don't always feel the need to say "please" when they tell you to do something. They may receive a report that you worked on all night without the slightest indication of gratitude. They may answer your request with a gruff

"No" without feeling any need to explain. They may be indifferent to the problems you have overcome. (A boss in my youth had a sign on the wall reading, "Don't tell me about the storms at sea. Just tell me when the ship's coming in.") So if you think you have a bad boss, first go to a quiet room, look deep into your soul, and determine whether you are a victim or a self-absorbed naïf. Which leads to the next tip:

10. The unentitled shall inherit the earth. - *Entitlement*

Many curmudgeons believe that a malady afflicts many of today's twenty-somethings: their sense of entitlement. It is their impression that too many of you think doing routine office tasks is beneath you, and your supervisors are insufficiently sensitive to your needs. Curmudgeons are also likely to think that you have a higher opinion of your abilities than your performance warrants.

To some extent, this is the age-old assumption that the younger generation has gone to the dogs ("When I was a kid, I walked five miles to school through snow-drifts six feet high"). But what people don't notice about such grumbling is that there is often truth in it. For example, none of my four children ever walked to school. I did routinely walk to school, but it was only two blocks for elementary school and about a mile for the higher grades, and my parents often drove me if the weather was bad. My parents grew up in rural Missouri, walking miles to school, through snowdrifts when necessary.

The same thing goes for jobs. Many of your supervisors in their fifties and older were getting up at five in the morning to deliver newspapers when they were nine or ten. In their teens, they babysat, clerked in stores, and, yes, flipped burgers. Many of them did hard physical work—they detasseled corn in the heat of August, worked construction, laid pipe, and painted houses. Many of them held jobs throughout college.

Some of you have held the same kind of jobs and know exactly what I'm talking about. In that case, I would be surprised if you have a problem with a sense of entitlement. Having done menial work in the past probably keeps you from feeling that some kinds of tasks are beneath you.

Now for those of you who have not held such jobs: As you look around at the behavior and conversation among your contemporaries at the office, can you see what I mean by "a sense of entitlement"? If you can't, maybe you're in an office where it truly isn't a problem. But there's an old saying among poker players: If you're at the table for more than half an hour and can't tell who the sucker is, you're it. Similarly, if you're a college graduate in your early twenties, and you look around at your peers and can't see a problem with a sense of entitlement, maybe you have a problem.

Curmudgeons are also irritated by the complaints they hear about today's job market, as if in the olden days every college graduate went directly to a meaningful job with a career ladder. When the curmudgeons in your life were twenty-two, most of them found that getting started in the job market was characterized by low pay, boring entry-level work, little job security, and promotions that had to be hard-earned. They don't see why you should feel like you are being subjected to some unprecedentedly harsh entry-level environment.

Curmudgeons think that the twenty-somethings' good opinion of themselves is especially inflated among graduates of elite colleges. Here's what the CEO of a large corporation said to me when the topic came up: "We don't even recruit at Harvard or Princeton anymore. We want kids from places like Southeastern Oklahoma State who have worked hard all their lives and share our values."

So be advised that curmudgeons are hypersensitive to any vibe that you give off when you're told to go pick up something in the mailroom. You don't have to say anything, or even roll your eyes. The slightest of sighs will lodge in their memory like their first kiss, only in a bad way.

11. Manners at the office and in general.

The sense of entitlement that many curmudgeons think your generation displays is part of a broader problem that I will call the It's All About Me Syndrome.

Let me begin by saying emphatically that the baby boomers are to blame. We started it fifty years ago, as we grew to adulthood in the 1960s convinced that we were the center of the universe and infinitely wiser than people over thirty. But for you as for us boomers, it is self-absorption: "Everything that happens is to be assessed first in terms of how I react to it and how it affects me."

In the half century since the first boomers came of age, demographic and economic trends have fed the problem. More young adults now have grown up as the only child in the family, never having had to share their parents' attention and get along with siblings. Increasing affluence has meant that adolescents with siblings often reach college without ever having shared a bedroom with another person, maybe not even a bathroom. The isolating effects of the IT revolution may contribute to the It's All About Me Syndrome—we spend more of our time in front of a screen and less with people. The strangers we encounter on the web are abstractions, not a physical presence—we are interfacing with them, not interacting.

The syndrome is reflected in the deterioration of manners. Deliberate rudeness is probably nonexistent in the office where you work, or so rare that it comes as a shock when it occurs, but *negligent* rudeness seems to be getting more common—things like people blocking the hall while they converse and not noticing that someone needs to get by, loud talking in places where the talkers should notice that others are trying to work, monopolizing cramped spaces such as the coffee room when others are waiting to get their coffee. It happens in public too—people talking loudly on cell phones, oblivious to how this intrudes on people nearby, not noticing (or pretending not to notice) that they're cutting into a line, not offering their bus or subway seat to someone who needs it more than they do.

But I'm trying to get at more subtle deteriorations of manners that constitute a retreat from graciousness. Let me give you a small example, but one worth pondering. For the last few decades, the informal way to respond to a request and to acknowledge a thank-you has become "no problem." As a response to a thank-you, I don't have a problem with "no problem." It is echoed in *"de rien,"* *"de nada,"* and informal thank-yous in many other languages. In Thai, the *only* expression for "thank you" translates as "it is not anything." But in response to a request, compare "no problem" with the ways in which people used to respond to a request: "I'll be happy to help," "my pleasure," "glad to help," or the elegant form, "it will be my pleasure." What's the difference between those alternatives to "no problem"? The alternatives express some form of pleasure in being able to respond to your request. When you unpack "No problem," what people are saying is "I can do what you've asked because it will not unduly burden me."

Some of you are rolling your eyes. After all, people don't really mean that they take pleasure in responding to someone's request. They're just saying it. "No problem" is actually a lot more honest, and it sounds breezy and cheerful. For that matter, "my pleasure" is hypocrisy when we're talking about someone who is getting paid to wait on someone else.

There's some truth to all that. But this much is certain: "It will be my pleasure" and its informal versions are all gracious. "No problem" is not. Graciousness is good. It is more pleasant to live in a world where people are gracious. And that brings me to the impoverished conception of *manners* with which most of us have been living for many decades.

In essence, good manners now consist of saying "Please," "Thank you," and "Excuse me" at frequent intervals, which almost all of us do. You know without doubt just how impoverished a conception this is if you have ever met a person with great manners. It is unlikely you have. Since the 1960s, people with great manners have been as rare as the ivory-billed wood-pecker. The two who have embodied great manners for me have been William F. Buckley, Jr., the late conservative writer, and his brother James, a former senator and retired judge.

What made their manners stand out? Nothing complicated. The two of the ten Buckley siblings I knew simply did all the little things that go into manners formally defined with the ease that comes from a lifetime of practice, and thereby made people who were in their presence feel as if they mattered.

Take, for example, the fading custom of rising when someone comes into a room. Most of us who still occasionally stand do so after a few seconds' delay, and awkwardly. There's a palpable sense of people remembering, *Oh yes, we're supposed to stand up now.* But the intended purpose of the gesture is to be welcoming, and that's how both Buckleys always did it—they were instantly, happily on their feet, accompanying the gesture with a smile and a few words that made you feel as if they had been waiting for the pleasure of seeing you arrive. They brought the same kind of ease to opening doors for others, rushing to get a chair when a newcomer was without one, or making sure to include someone in the conversation who seemed shy. Hypocrisy? You can try to tell me that, but it sure felt like a

warm bubble bath of good fellowship to the people who were lucky enough to be in their company.

Here's the problem: I'm not sure any of us can acquire great manners as adults. I'm confident that as little boys the Buckley brothers were systematically instructed on the proper way to behave in all situations and were continually admonished and corrected until they got it right, all the time (absent that kind of training, it would be too much of a coincidence that they were both so perfectly good at the same things). They added a lot of natural charm and good nature to that instruction, but I'm afraid that the systematic instruction is necessary—instruction I didn't get as a child and that I did not provide for my children. I was taught to be polite, and I helped my wife teach our children to be polite. We didn't teach them to have great manners in the way that it probably has to be systematically taught.

So what can you do if you too were taught to be polite but not put through the childhood instruction that goes into great manners? Maybe there's nothing you can do right away. But here's a possibility: If you have children, how about instructing them? You wouldn't be the first person who learned how to do something by teaching it.

Meanwhile, you can do something about the sins of obliviousness that are fed by the It's All About Me Syndrome. You're supposed to notice that somebody's

trying to get past you in the hall, that others nearby are trying to work, that the woman who just got on the subway car is pregnant and needs a place to sit, and take the initiative to do the right thing.

"It's all about me" is a form of solipsism. Even though the boomers started it, it's time for your generation to end it. Practice continual situational awareness, react according to how that situation is affecting others around you, and fight the temptation to think first about how things affect you. While you're at it, take your situational awareness a step further and practice humility in the sense that C. S. Lewis meant it in his aphorism: "Humility is not thinking less of yourself. It's thinking of yourself less."

12. Standing out isn't as hard as you think (I).

When I was in my twenties, I worried about whether I would ever get the big break that I thought was necessary for rising to the top. Without doubt, breaks can be important, but they aren't as important as I thought then. Looking at it from the bottom, I saw the people on top as having an unlimited number of good people to hire and promote, among whom I was helplessly anonymous. It was only many years later that I discovered it looks completely different from the top. Good help is

hard to find. *Really* hard to find. Sure, there are lots of people with the right degrees and résumés, but the kind of employee we yearn for sticks out almost immediately.

If you are that person, the first and most obvious way you stick out is by working long hours. I don't mean that you cheerfully say "yes" when your boss asks you to work late. You don't lose points by doing so (whereas saying "no" amounts to self-immolation), but what we curmudgeons treasure are employees who figure out for themselves that the task of the moment requires long hours to complete, and stay as long as necessary without having to be asked.

I'm not talking about make-work or about long hours for the sake of long hours. In a purposeful organization run by good people, there's always more useful work than can be done in an eight-hour workday. That doesn't mean that the additional useful work must get done right away. Some of it must; some of it can wait. As you get older and acquire a spouse and children, you learn to limit yourself to what *must* get done so that you don't wake up at age sixty and realize you haven't had a life outside work. But at age twenty-five, say, without a spouse or children, you have a lot more freedom to throw yourself into your work, and in doing so to impress the curmudgeons. Or, you can try to lead a balanced life even when you're twenty-five. It's your choice.

Though why anyone would want to lead a balanced life at twenty-five is beyond me.

If you are indeed working in a purposeful organization run by good people, I assure you: It will get you noticed, assuming you are also competent. Rising in an organization doesn't require breaks if you are competent and work hard enough. Here's the secret you should remember whenever you hear someone lamenting how tough it is to get ahead in the postindustrial global economy: Few people work nearly as hard as they could. The few who do have it made.

13. Standing out isn't as hard as you think (II).

One of the key men who got America to the moon was George Low, the head of the program that produced the Apollo spacecraft. When my wife and I were writing a book about the Apollo program, one of his colleagues described Low to us this way: "George was the kind of guy who if you gave him a job emptying wastebaskets, he would stretch it into overtime, not because he was loafing, but because he'd find more to emptying wastebaskets than you ever imagined could be there." And therein lies another reason that standing out from the crowd isn't as hard as you think. You can be sitting in a quite junior job, be given a routine assignment, and still make a big impression. Let me tell you a story.

In the early 1990s, during the research for a book that was eventually published as *The Bell Curve*, I was given part of the time of a research assistant. Call this person Irene. I gave Irene the assignment of digging up data on pre-1950 college entrance test scores. It was an unexciting assignment, and I didn't expect much to come of it.

Irene disappeared for a week or so and returned with the mother lode—a rich assortment of data that I had no idea existed, from incredibly obscure sources, that would open up entirely new topics in the chapter I was writing. How did she do it? I don't know the details, but I'm sure it consisted of going from the easy stuff—articles in the major technical journals—to the sources they used, then going to that second tier and searching out the sources *they* used. That's the way it's done—unravel that sock all the way down to the last thread. She had simply done it more thoroughly and with more impressive results than I had thought possible.

I was dazzled, and let it be known to the senior staff of AEI that Irene was hot stuff. About four years later I decided to embark on a big new project. I hadn't even seen Irene in the interim. But I knew what a massive research task I was facing, so it was Irene who came to mind. I got hold of her and offered her full coauthor-ship on the forthcoming book if she joined me in the ef-fort. As it happens, Irene had just gotten the job offer of her dreams elsewhere, and she turned me down. Still, my making the offer is evidence of the rewards that a terrific job on a routine assignment can lead to. Supe-rior performance is extremely rare, and it stands out. That statement applies to every job in the organization, no matter how junior.

Furthermore, you should keep in mind that the people who are most likely to recognize superior per-formance are successful curmudgeons. Suppose you are stuck with a job as an administrative assistant and want to break out into a managerial career track. If that's your ambition, you don't want to be assigned to a friendly, sympathetic boss who forgives his assis-tant's mistakes. You want to be assigned to a success-ful curmudgeon, the more demanding the better. He is more likely to have a gimlet eye for mistakes—and by the same token is more likely to notice when they *don't* occur. Being successful himself, he is likely to be in love with excellent performance and to be impressed when he detects it. Curmudgeons have their faults, but if you can sneak past our crotchets and get hired, we are your best bet to become your self-appointed advocates if you perform at a high level.

ON THINKING AND WRITING WELL

Part of healthy ambition is the desire to achieve excellence as a practitioner of your craft. I cannot be of any help about the specifics of your craft, but my own profession as a social scientist who writes for a general audience involves a craft that is almost surely an important component of your job: writing. Only a few of you will write professionally as I do. But many of you will be in occupations that require you to write reports or briefs or memos. Writing well won't necessarily push you up the ladder, but writing badly can keep you from rising. It's no use being a clear thinker if you cannot communicate those thoughts. More important: Unless you're in the hard sciences, *the process of writing is your most valuable single tool for developing better ideas. The process of writing is the dominant source of intellectual creativity.*

14. Putting together your basic writing toolkit.

Before the writing process can do these great things, you need to put together your toolkit. A few resources must always be within reach when you write.

The Elements of Style **by William Strunk, Jr., and E. B. White.** It has been fashionable for some years to trash *The Elements of Style*, but it's still a fine little book. No, you don't always want to write as sparely as Strunk and White advise—*after* you have mastered the principles of clean, clear prose that Strunk and White teach. William Zinsser's *On Writing Well* is an excellent book designed to be the next step after you've absorbed the lessons of *The Elements of Style*.

A dictionary and a thesaurus. In this era, online versions are fine. Since they're so easy to access, use overkill—if you have the slightest doubt about the nuances of a word's meaning, check a couple of definitions. Use an online thesaurus whenever you have the slightest sense that you could find a better word than the one you're using. "The difference between the almost right word and the right word is really a large matter," Mark Twain wrote. "It's the difference between the lightning bug and the lightning." He was right. The substitution of exactly the right word can transform a sentence. The difference between okay writing and good writing is the sum of dozens of such small improvements. But don't just pick a word at random from the choices the thesaurus gives you. All of the words in that list have different shades of meaning. You need to pick the one that means *exactly* what you're trying to convey. Which brings us to usage.

Good references on usage. Bookmark the website "Common Errors in English Usage" (http://public.wsu.edu/~brians/errors/errors.html). It is a good source and convenient. But *Woe Is I* by Patricia T. O'Conner is more fun. She has a companion book, *Words Fail Me*, which I also recommend. Add Lynne Truss's *Eats, Shoots and Leaves* on punctuation. All of these books lend themselves to browsing, but you really need to read them from cover to cover. Even a single important error in usage registers with curmudgeons.

You should also have the most recent version of *Fowler's Modern English Usage* within a few feet of your computer, but *Fowler's* is a reference book that you're likely to pick up only when you have a specific question in mind. For professional writers, the *Chicago Manual of Style* is also a must.

Someone to imitate. This doesn't count as part of your toolkit, but it is a useful tool for learning to write: Imitate. Near the beginning of my career, I had a boss, Paul Schwarz, who wrote slightly eccentric but elegant prose. During the first few years I worked for him, I consciously tried to write just like he did. I'm sure doing so produced some laughably bad work at the beginning, but by the end my writing had improved a lot. If you aren't lucky enough to have someone to imitate in your life, choose the best writers in your line of work and try to imitate their style. James Q. Wilson and Irving Kristol have been other models for me.

15. A bare-bones usage primer.

The short primer that follows is no substitute for studying a good book on English usage, but it will get you started. It begins with a list of the serious errors that may instantly lead a curmudgeon to pigeonhole you as hopeless, then moves on to lists of other pairs of words with importantly distinct meanings, words and phrases that you should never use, and pairs of words with spelling so close that you have to beware of confusing them.

The Surely Injurious and Possibly Fatal Errors Plus a Few Niceties

If you Google the following errors in usage, you will often find impressive authorities telling you to never mind, usage has evolved, these distinctions are no longer important, relax. That attitude applies to almost everybody you encounter—except, quite possibly, the person on whose good opinion your future depends. I have put the errors in rough order from the ones I consider fatal to more survivable ones.

Disinterested used to mean *uninterested*. The meaning of *disinterested* is "free of bias and self-interest." It is essential that a judge be disinterested, for example. *Disinterested* does NOT, repeat NOT, mean "lack of interest" or "uninterested." I put this so emphatically because we're not talking just about proper usage. *Disinterest* used in its correct sense is on its last legs—I've been appalled to see it misused in articles in the *Washington Post* and other major publications. English does not have another word that conveys the meaning of *disinterested* as economically. If we lose the distinctive meaning of the word, we have measurably degraded our ability to express ourselves in English.

Literally used to mean *figuratively*. The percentage of times that *literally* is used correctly verges on zero. Ninety-nine percent of the time (I'm estimating), it is misused to mean *figuratively*. In almost all of the other one percent, *literally* is used as a sloppy intensifier. The only correct use of *literally* that comes to mind is the sign-off of George Burns and Gracie Allen, former vaudevillians who had a television sitcom in the 1950s. She played the role of a ditz. At the end of the show, George would say, "Say good night, Gracie," and she would say, "Good night, Gracie." She took George's instruction literally. Such opportunities to use *literally* correctly don't come up often.

Confusing *can* and *may*. *Can* refers to the possibility of doing something, whereas *may* refers to permission to do something. It's an important distinction, worth preserving (see tip #26). Do your part.

Using *which* instead of *that*. *That* introduces essential clauses while *which* introduces nonessential clauses. Consider the sentence "Tools that have sharp edges can cause nasty cuts." If you remove the words "that have sharp edges," the sentence loses much of its meaning. The clause is essential. Now consider "Roses, which come in many colors, have thorns on their stems." You can remove "which come in many colors" and the meaning of the rest of the sentence is intact. The clause is not essential. Another way to remember: If the clause obviously needs to be set off by commas, use *which*.

Mistakenly putting an apostrophe in *its*. I make this error all the time when I'm writing a first draft—putting in an apostrophe when you're using the possessive case is so natural that it's hard to resist. But it looks bad once it's on paper or the screen. You want to correct this natural mistake before you hit the send button or submit something for distribution. *It's* with the apostrophe is the contraction of *it is*. If you are using the possessive case of *its*, there's no apostrophe.

The misplacement of *only*. The word *only* should immediately precede the word or phrase it modifies. Consider the three different meanings of these sentences:

> I saw only the collision.
> I only saw the collision.
> Only I saw the collision.

In everyday speech, almost all of us are sloppy about this one, but be careful when you are writing. Putting *only* in the right place will at least eliminate ambiguities and sometimes prevent an outright misunderstanding of what you mean.

Confusing *affect* with *effect*. Do you immediately know the differences in what the following four sentences mean?

> Her action affected the decision.
> Her action effected the decision.
> She told me she loved me without effect.
> She told me she loved me without affect.

If the answer is no, you have some work to do. The rule of thumb is that for the great majority of times you want to use these words, *effect* is the noun and *affect* (to have an effect on) is the verb. Only rarely will you have occasion to use *effect* as a verb or *affect* as a noun, but you need to know the different meanings of *effect* and *affect* lest you blot your copybook.

Unique used to mean unusual. If something is unique, it is one of a kind. Something cannot be *somewhat unique* or *very unique*. That doesn't mean you can never modify *unique*. For example, something can be *almost unique* or *unequivocally unique*. Just don't use an adjective that ignores the core meaning of "one of a kind."

Center around. What could this possibly mean? The center can be only one point. You mean *center on* or *revolve around*.

One of the only. Another common phrase in spoken English that makes no sense when you stop to think about it. Use "one of the few" when you're writing.

General consensus. Redundant. *Consensus* means general agreement.

Whether or not. Usually redundant. Try deleting *or not* and see if the sentence still makes sense.

Confusing *farther* with *further*. *Farther* involves physical distance whereas *further* does not. You travel farther, but you decide something upon further consideration. The mnemonic is that *farther* contains the word *far*.

Confusing *less* with *fewer*. When you are referring to an amount, use *less*. When you are referring to a number of things, use *fewer*. You drink less milk, but drink fewer glasses of milk. Why then do we usually refer to "less than five hours" instead of "fewer than five hours"? Because usually we are talking about an amount of time, not a number of hours.

Confusing *amount* with *number*. Parallels *less* and *fewer*. You have an *amount* of money but a *number* of dollars.

Confusing *over* with *more* and *under* with *less*. The same family of errors. In spoken language, there's no harm in saying "the bill was over $100." When writing, use *more than*.

***Fortuitous* used to mean *fortunate* or *serendipitous*.** *Fortuitous* means happening by accident or chance. It has no good (or bad) connotations. *Serendipitous* means the faculty of making fortunate discoveries by accident. So Alexander Fleming's discovery of penicillin because he mistakenly left a petri dish open overnight was both fortuitous and serendipitous.

***Dilemma* used to mean *difficult decision*.** Not all difficult decisions are dilemmas. A dilemma (from the Greek word meaning "double proposition") refers to a situation in which a choice must be made between two undesirable alternatives.

***Masterful* used to mean *masterly*.** When people use *masterful*, they almost always really mean *masterly*: performing in an extremely skillful and accomplished way. As in the case of *disinterested*, we are in danger of losing a useful word for which we have no ready alternative. If you want to describe someone who exhibits the qualities of a person who is confidently and effectively in authority, with connotations of power and dominance, *masterful* is the perfect word. Use *masterly* when you want to compliment someone for exhibiting a high level of skill.

Orders of magnitude and quantum leap used to mean a lot. *Orders of magnitude* refer to powers of ten. To increase by one order of magnitude is to increase tenfold; to increase by two orders of magnitude is to increase a hundredfold. You seldom want to convey to your reader that something increased even tenfold, let alone a hundredfold, which means that you should seldom use *order of magnitude*. A quantum leap refers to a sudden change in state, not to an increase in anything. If you're tempted to use *quantum leap*, you probably have in mind a *qualitative increase*.

Confusing *comprise* with *constitute, consist,* or *compose*. The word *comprise* is distinct from the alternatives in that it refers to the components of something from the point of view of the whole: the whole *comprises* the parts. So the United States *comprises* fifty states. But you can also choose to say that the whole *consists of* the parts, the whole is *composed of* the parts, or the whole is *constituted of* the parts. What you want to avoid is writing that something is *comprised of* the parts.

Problematic used to mean "I have a problem with this." Something is problematic if it is difficult to resolve or if it presents an objective problem that needs to be resolved. It doesn't mean that you personally have an objection to something. For example, it is appropriate to say that a proposed voter ID bill is problematic because it risks disenfranchising more eligible voters than it prevents fraudulent votes, but not to say that it is problematic because it is racist and offensive. That may be your sincere opinion, but people on the other side can be just as sincerely convinced that it is not racist and offensive and neither side can prove the other wrong. I should add that I've been guilty of this misuse of *problematic*. It's a seductively attractive way to introduce a personal opinion without having to take responsibility for it.

Using *concerted effort* when only one person is involved. By definition, a concerted effort can be made only by more than one person.

Begs the question used to mean *raises the question, evades the question,* or *makes you wonder.* To beg the question means to assume as true the thing that you are trying to prove—to make an unsupported claim with circular reasoning. The tip-off is that a person who has begged the question has in effect repeated himself. A classic example used to illustrate *begging the question* is "Opium induces sleep because it has a soporific quality." Like *literally, beg the question* is almost never used correctly. It usually would be more accurate to say that someone has raised the question, evaded the question, or made you wonder about something.

Notorious used to mean *famous.* *Notorious* means famous in a bad way. Never use *notorious* to describe someone who is famous for acceptable reasons. Lance Armstrong was a famous bicyclist who became notorious for his lies about doping. While I'm on the subject: *Notorious* is not as evil or horrible as *infamous.* Armstrong is notorious. Hitler, Mao, and Stalin were infamous.

Decimate used to mean *destroy* **or** *inflict great damage.* You don't need to worry about this one unless you're dealing with someone who is not only a curmudgeon but even more pedantic than I am. The primary meaning of *decimate* is now indeed *destroy* or *inflict great damage.* But it originated in Roman times and referred to a punishment in which a tenth of the members of an army unit were executed. Once you're aware of that, it's hard to read someone's use of *decimate* to mean *destroy* without remembering that it really means destruction of only a tenth of the whole.

Confusing *continual* **with** *continuous.* Nobody will get upset if you use these two words interchangeably, but I like this example of how precise English can be. *Continual* means that something happens repeatedly; *continuous* means that something happens without interruption. It is a useful distinction—and I guarantee that you can remember which is which: The last three letters of *continuous* are *ous*. One Unbroken Sequence. You'll never forget it.

Words with Distinctive Meanings You Ought to Check Out

Mistakes with the following sets of words don't pose nearly the same danger of a catastrophic curmudgeon eruption as using *disinterested* to mean *uninterested*, but you should at least be aware that the words in each set don't mean the same thing. I couldn't describe all of the distinctions to you off the top of my head, but I know enough to go to a dictionary whenever I'm about to use one of them in written work. That's what you should aim for: an internal alarm bell.

abstruse/obtuse

accurate/precise

adage/aphorism/maxim

adverse/averse

agnostic/atheist

ambiguous/ambivalent

amoral/immoral

attain/obtain

avocation/vocation

axiom/premise

barter/haggle

biannual/biennial

biweekly/semiweekly

both/each

celebrated/illustrious/famous

celibate/chaste

ceremonial/ceremonious

conflicted/conflicting

convince/persuade

credible/credulous

crescendo/climax

critique/criticize

degrade/denigrate

derisory/derisive

differ/vary

diplomatic/tactful

dispose/dispose of

dissemble/lie

dogma/doctrine

duress/stress

empathy/sympathy

emulate/imitate

endemic/epidemic

envious/jealous

explicitly/implicitly

flaunt/flout

forbidding/formidable

forceful/forcible/forced

goal/objective

hardy/hearty

hero/protagonist

impeach/impugn

induce/deduce

luxuriant/luxurious

majority/plurality

nauseous/nauseated

obdurate/stubborn

oblige/obligate

obsolescent/obsolete

occupy/preoccupy

oppress/repress

oral/verbal

peruse/skim

perverse/perverted

practicable/practical

precipitate/precipitous

predominate/predominant

presently/currently

rebut/refute

regretfully/regrettably

reluctant/reticent

rob/steal

sarcastic/ironic

seduce/tempt

sensual/sensuous

stand/stance

vapid/vacuous

vehement/voluble

Words and Phrases That Are Wrong or Don't Really Exist (or Exist Only Because We Live in a Degraded Age)

doubtlessly	much differently
impactful	overexaggerated
irregardless	perogative
mischievious	predominately

Pairs of Words with Close Spellings That Must Not Be Interchanged in Written English

These are pairs of words with different meanings that are familiar to you, I'm sure (if not, you really need to hit the English usage books), but with spellings so similar you might wrongly substitute one for another in written language. Many of them are homophones. Run your eye over the list to see if any pose potential problems for you. A spell checker won't catch these if you make a mistake.

alliterate/illiterate	arrant/errant
allusion/illusion	ascent/assent
alter/altar	aural/oral
appraise/apprise	baldfaced/boldfaced

born/borne

breach/breech

canvas/canvass

complimentary/
complementary

confident/confidant

defuse/diffuse

demur/demure

desert/dessert

discreet/discrete

gaff/gaffe

gibe/jibe

grisly/grizzly

hanger/hangar

incidence/incidents

indite/indict

loath/loathe

mantel/mantle

precedence/precedents

preemptory/peremptory

prostrate/prostate

rational/rationale

role/roll

stationary/stationery

16. Writing when you already know what you want to say.

This tip is about the writing we do every day—a memorandum, a progress report, maybe an important email—that needs to be written well but does not require a creative thought. We pretty much know what we want to say before we begin.

But knowing what you want to say is not the same as expressing it well. You are trying to make a point. That means a logical, persuasive train of thought and the right language for expressing it. Hardly anyone gets it right in the first draft. I certainly don't. I'm not a good writer. I don't show my first drafts to anyone because they are embarrassingly bad. But I'm a good rewriter. Here's how I go about it.

Getting started. I never approach the first draft saying to myself, "Just slap your thoughts down quickly and then go back and fix the prose." Whenever I've tried to do that, I've ended up with an unusable mess. I suspend disbelief and assume with each click of the keys that I'm writing a sentence that will stick. Doing so doesn't mean I get to the end of a sentence before changing it. All the typing I did on the first two paragraphs of this tip would have taken up more than a full page, and all of it would have consisted of changes I kept making in sentences as I went along. There were several false starts, but usually I didn't get to even the end of the sentence before realizing it was a false start. After about half an hour I got to the point I intended: Right now, those first two paragraphs look okay to me. It's plausible that they will remain close to their present form in the final version.

"Plausible" is enough. I know from experience that there's a good chance that major chunks of the first two paragraphs won't survive, but right now I feel as if I'm on the right track, and that's the crucial thing. *If you have the sense that an earlier part of your piece is wrong, don't try to plow ahead. Go back and fix what's wrong.*

Always be reasonably satisfied with the draft up to the point at which you're typing.

Talk to yourself. My wife says that sometimes my lips move as I write. Even when they don't, I'm always silently vocalizing my words. The easiest way to identify clunkiness in your prose is to hear it, out loud or in your head. The awkward phrase or the clumsy Latinate word becomes obvious. It *sounds* clunky. Right now, for example, I'm still fretting over the phrase "I know from experience that there's a good chance . . ." in the preceding paragraph. The "that there's" combination sounds clunky and is driving me crazy. I'll probably leave it unchanged so I can use it as an illustration. Otherwise, I'd go back and fix it.

Constantly reread. A certain degree of infatuation with your own stuff is helpful in writing well. The writer who enjoys reading his own sentences over and over but who is also self-critical will endlessly tweak his work—a word change here, shifting a few words around there, playing with punctuation—and it will be improved in the process. Constantly rereading while you're working on a draft also helps keep your presentation focused and consistent. If you don't reread, you're much more likely to drift off course.

"Kill your darlings." That's William Faulkner's version, and the one most often quoted, but the observation originally comes from the English writer and literary critic Arthur Quiller-Couch in his essay "On Style." He wrote, "Whenever you feel an impulse to perpetrate a piece of exceptionally fine writing, obey it—whole-heartedly—and delete it before sending your manuscript to press. Murder your darlings."

It has happened to me many times. I write a sentence or paragraph that I'm extremely proud of. It's way above my usual expressiveness, nuance, and imagination. I just love it. Then a still, small voice says to me, "It doesn't belong." My impulse is to respond, "Who cares if it doesn't belong? It's *great*." But the still, small voice is right. You'll know it when it happens to you. Delete it. Mourn it, but delete it. Ernest Hemingway had a companion observation about writing: "The most essential gift for a good writer is a built-in, shock-proof, shit detector."

Edit the piece in hard copy before sending out the final version. I have done my writing and editing on a computer screen since the last half of the 1970s. But even after more than thirty years of using a computer to write and edit, this truth remains: When I read a hard copy of text, I see things I haven't seen on the computer screen. It never, ever fails. Don't send out anything until you have printed it out and edited the paper version of your text with a pen or pencil.

Do a final check of your adjectives and adverbs and a global deletion of "very." You will be surprised how often adjectives and adverbs have made your prose mushier instead of more expressive. As for *very*, you may, if you insist, take a look at each occurrence before deleting. But hardly any of them should survive.

Let the final draft cool overnight. Whenever I have finished a short piece of work, have edited it, and think it looks ready to send out, an evil spirit (not the still, small voice) says to me, "I know what you always say, but trust me, this piece is just fine. It's ready to go. Send it out and get on to something else." The evil spirit is always wrong. When I wait to look over the piece the next morning, I always find improvements, sometimes crucial improvements, that I didn't see when I first thought I was finished.

There's no mystery to this. Writing is not a unitary thing. Even a piece of less than a thousand words has dozens of moving parts, and it is not within the scope of the human mind, or at least my human mind, to review all those moving parts consciously and at one time. And so while watching a TV show the evening after finishing the piece, a word or phrase will pop into my head that works much better than the one I used in the afternoon. At three in the morning, I will suddenly awaken and realize to my horror that there's an obvious lacuna in my argument—so obvious that it's inconceivable I could have missed it. But I did, and, by letting the final draft cool overnight, found it.

17. Writing when you don't know what you want to say.

The previous tip was about technique. This tip gets to the essence of intellectual creativity in fields in which creativity is expressed in words, not mathematics or images.

The situation: You have collected information involving questions to which you didn't know all the answers before you began, and you are now supposed to relate what you have learned to an audience of readers. That's the situation I face when I am in the writing stage of a book project, but it's also the situation that you will face in a career in academia, the law, journalism, politics, or business, as you are called upon to write reports, memoranda, briefs, or articles.

Here's the first rule: *Don't assume that you are aware of all you know before you have written it.* No one can think through all the implications of a complicated body of information before putting a word on paper, any more than one can think through how all the pieces of a jigsaw puzzle will fit together when they are spread out on a table.

The act of beginning the text involves suspension of disbelief again. Just as you have to write each sentence as if it is final draft, even though you know that it probably will not survive, you also have to start writing as if you know what you know, even though you realize that your thinking is going to change, perhaps radically, as you go along. These are the strategies that work for me:

The less you know what you want to say, the more non-linear the writing process becomes. If you're trying to figure out what you think as you write, it's common to find that you've changed your mind about what you really meant three sentences earlier. Go back and fix that sentence, which then lets you improve the last sentence. After you've improved the last sentence, you'll realize you need to tweak the intervening sentences as well. Don't get frustrated if it takes you a long time to get from one paragraph to the next. It's a healthy sign that you're engaged in creative interaction with your material.

Rereading is your primary tool for unfolding your insights. Rereading is an excellent way to improve your prose, but it is even more valuable as a way to improve your thought. Every time you open the document you've been working on, reread what you've written (if you're working on a book, start at the beginning of the current chapter). Don't bear down, consciously scrutinizing each word. Just skate over the text until your eye catches something that could be said better, and stop to fix it. It might be as simple as replacing a single word, but often it's something more significant. Here are three things to look for (you'll do this unconsciously after you've been at it long enough):

1. *The sentences aren't in the right order.* One symptom of a thought that's not fully formed is that when you first write it down, you don't get the logical order right. Without realizing it, you've blurted out step #3 without having written down steps #1 and #2, and then (still without realizing it) you put down a few sentences that express steps #1 and #2 in a confused way. As you start to rearrange the sentences into a more logical presentation, you will commonly find that not only are you doing a better job of expressing your argument, but the argument itself has evolved and gotten richer.

2. *A sentence has more in it than one sentence can hold.* My internalized label for this is "packed" sentences. Your eye is skimming along the text and stops because the sentence is too hard to read. It's convoluted or opaque. You start to fix it as you would fix any other clunky sentence, just to improve the prose, but then you realize *why* the sentence needs fixing: You're really trying to say more than one thing, or you're saying one thing too telegraphically, and you shouldn't have crammed it into one sentence. As you explicate your thought, it turns out that the solution isn't two sentences instead of one. You have a whole new paragraph, or two paragraphs, or two pages, or more. Once again,

not only have the changes expressed your original argument more clearly, but your argument has evolved and deepened.

3. *The transition between paragraphs is rough.* You're skimming along the text, just taking in the flow, and you stop because you notice that the first sentence of a paragraph doesn't quite follow from the last sentence of the preceding paragraph. So you stop to rewrite—and then you realize that the problem isn't in the wording of either sentence, but instead reflects something you've left out. So you start to add the missing piece to smooth the transition.

Of all the ways in which rereading leads to creative thought, fixing rough transitions between paragraphs is probably the most consistently productive. There's no telling how much new material will come flowing out of you. Years ago, I was talking about this with the late Richard Herrnstein while we were working on *The Bell Curve.* "Yes," Dick said, "I remember once when I noticed a rough transition between paragraphs. By the time I fixed it, I had seven new chapters."

I've given you three specific things to look for as you reread. I hope they will be useful, but the main thing to remember is the frame of mind common to all three. Enjoy your own writing, but cheerfully take for granted that you're always going to find things that need fixing, and take pleasure in fixing them as you find them.

And then the next day reread again. How do you know when the piece is finished? When you read all the way through, in hard copy, without finding a single thing you want to change.

I've left out one other way of coming up with new insights, because there's not much to be said about it. Every once in a while—maybe only a few times over the course of a major project; sometimes zero times—you will be writing easily, in the zone, your fingers tapping away on the keys. Then you hit the period on a sentence and are jolted to a stop. You reread what you've just typed and you say to yourself, "Where did *that* come from?" A line of thought that had never occurred to you has dropped onto your text from somewhere mysterious, and you know instantly that it will prove to be a vein of pure gold. Not much about writing is magical. Those moments are.

Don't count on them.

18. Don't wait for the muse.

The last of my tips about writing is simple and absolute: Don't wait until you feel like it. Find out what time of day you write best and develop a routine that puts you in front of your keyboard and screen at whatever time that might be.

I'm a morning person, so I'm up by 6:30 and usually sitting at my computer before 7:00. By 11:00, I have usually stopped writing first draft. I can edit existing draft or do data analysis indefinitely, but first draft takes something out of me. After a couple of hours of intense work, I look at the paragraph I'm struggling with and know that it will be easier to finish it tomorrow. Other writers who talk about their routines usually make the same point—three or four hours a day is about the maximum that can be expected.

What about the days when you can't face the prospect of putting new sentences on the screen? Turn to the great cure-all for all things pertaining to writing: reread. Mentally cut yourself some slack, agree not to try to do first draft, and set out to look at what you've got and make whatever edits occur to you. At worst, you'll be spending your time usefully. More commonly, you will get caught up in an edit that turns out to be more significant than a few tweaks, and you'll regain consciousness an hour later with some good new draft that you hadn't planned on writing. In other words, fool yourself into writing.

What do you do if you get writer's block? I've never suffered from it. From what I've read about the torments experienced by those who have, you had probably better get into another line of work. But first make sure that it's really writer's block. Probably you just don't feel like writing today, which takes us back to where we started: Don't wait until you feel like it.

19. Learn to love rigor.

I cannot offer specific techniques about how to think well apart from its connection to writing well, because "how to think well" in different professions involves such different disciplines. I spend much of my time conducting statistical analyses of large databases. Someone in the financial industry may also conduct statistical analyses of large databases, but using completely different techniques and applying different modes of analytical thought. "Thinking well" has equally diverse requirements for lawyers, physicians, journalists, marketing executives, and sitcom writers. But I can offer strategic advice that will do for your mental processes what the gym does for your body: Learn to love rigor. The dictionary meaning of *rigor* I have in mind is "the quality of being extremely thorough, exhaustive, or accurate."

If your major in college was anything except one of the hard sciences, you may not have experienced much demand to be rigorous up to this point in your life. How many of your teachers not only demanded that you write papers instead of taking multiple-choice tests, but handed back those papers with every error in syntax, usage, and spelling marked in red, and every error in logic pointed out? How often during class discussions have you been criticized for a sloppy argument, even though your conclusion may have been correct? Has any teacher ever drilled you on the major fallacies? Has any teacher ever drilled you on the principles of rhetoric? If you've had such experiences and remember them fondly, you're already susceptible to the delights of rigor—but such experiences are far too rare in today's universities.

What kind of instruction did you get in reaching sound judgments? Did your university require you to take courses in statistics? All of the important evidence on topics such as global warming, income inequality, the effects of secondhand smoke, or attempts to help disadvantaged children—topics that you probably have opinions about—is quantitative and statistical. No one can have *informed* opinions about such topics without being able to appraise the evidence, which in turn requires a thorough understanding of the nature of probability and its calibration.

What have you learned from your training in history? Pattern recognition is one reason that a thorough grounding in history was once seen as an indispensable part of a liberal education—why, in the words of George Santayana, those who cannot remember the past are condemned to repeat it. That's why the American founders systematically studied every historical example of a republic, so their Constitution could deal with the forces that had destroyed past republics. You probably have opinions about legalizing gay marriage, how Israel and the Palestinians should deal with their differences, and what the federal government should do about illegal immigration. But having an *informed* opinion about any of those issues requires knowledge of history that is both broad and deep—not because that knowledge will inevitably lead you to a particular position, but because you need to weigh the historical experience of advanced societies of the past—the experience most relevant to us—against your preferences that are based only on the facts of the current situation. What resemblance does this use of history bear to the amount of history, or the type of history, that you learned in college?

What kind of training did you have in literature, art, or music? Did your professors demand that you master the criteria for assessing excellence in each of those disciplines? Did you have to learn the hard stuff? Or perhaps you just read some fiction, looked at some pictures, listened to some music, and gave your opinions about them—opinions shaped by nothing except your personal preferences.

I'm sure there are exceptions among you. But even

those of you who are exceptions know that you are exceptions, and that graduates of even the most elite universities can leave school still innocent of what it means to be pushed to the limits of their intellectual potential. If you feel that's true of you, you're going to have to learn to push yourself. How do you do that? Having a curmudgeon for a boss is a good way to jump-start the process. Ultimately, you have to acquire a mind-set.

If you've been told to get information on some problem, you've got to want to get all the information you can possibly find on that problem.

If you've had to do some calculations in the course of an assignment, you've got to want to replicate the entire analysis from scratch before you hand in your results.

If an assignment leads you to half a dozen different options to explore, you've got to want to explore all of them, and not mind if you "waste" a lot of time determining that five of the six are dead ends.

As you start to reach conclusions about a problem, you've got to want to figure out why you might be wrong.

Note that I did not just say that you should *do* certain things, but that you must *want* to do them. That's what being in love with rigor means. It is at the heart of thinking well, and of the satisfactions you will take from your accomplishments.

ON THE FORMATION OF WHO YOU ARE

The years just after college can be predictable or transformative. They are predictable if your career plans are on rails. You're going to become a physician, let's say, so you take pre-med as an undergraduate and go directly to medical school. Little will be unpredictable. The same goes for the law, if you move directly from college to law school. It can be true even if you plan a business career. The top MBA programs now usually require a few years between undergraduate school and entry into the MBA program, so you go to work for a carefully selected business after you get your BA for one reason: to punch your work-experience ticket so you can get into Sloan or Wharton or HBS.

There's nothing morally defective about having such a fully developed plan. It just presumes that you know exactly what you want out of life before you're twenty-two years old. It forecloses doing anything else with your twenties, the time of life when you have the fewest responsibilities and will suffer the fewest penalties for mistakes and failures. That never appealed to me. Consider some ways in which your twenties can be transformative.

20. Leave home.

If you haven't left home already, it's time to jump out of the nest, and these days you can't count on parents to do the right thing and push you out. So jump even if they say you don't have to. You'll figure out how to fly before you hit the ground—not well, maybe, but you'll be flying.

Don't argue that you can't find a job that pays enough to support yourself. You can. You just can't find a job that will support you in the style to which you have been accustomed. So accustom yourself to a new style. Learn to get by on little—prove to yourself how resourceful you can be. Move out. No matter what.

And don't let your parents support you. It's okay if Mom or Dad gives you a loan so that you can make the required deposit when you rent an apartment. It's okay for them to give you birthday and Christmas checks that you and they both realize are not for buying yourself a present but to help keep you afloat. These are advantages that your contemporaries from less affluent families don't have, and they will retard your transition to full independence to some degree. But, at the least, you need to be paying your own rent, buying your own food, taking care of your own laundry—in a hundred ways, assuming responsibility for yourself. Many of you have parents who, for the most loving reasons, are willing to prolong your adolescence if you let them. Don't let them.

21. Recalibrate your perspective on time.

A common and depressing assumption on the part of many college students is that they must stay on the academic rails until they are professionally established—go directly to grad school from college and directly from grad school to a job, as if there were some big rush and even a few years lost would put them catastrophically behind everyone else.

Nonsense. Suppose you intend to retire at sixty-five. If you don't start your career until you're thirty, that still gives you thirty-five years to make it professionally. If you can't make it in thirty-five years, you weren't going to make it in forty or forty-five.

You probably won't really have to wait until you're thirty to begin your vocation. With any luck, you will have identified something you really want to do before then. But in general, think of your twenties as a time for doing the things that you won't be able to do when you have a spouse and children. There is only the stipulation from the previous tip: You have to support yourself. An essential part of the experience is being on your own.

If you are as ambitious as I was, the real barrier to treating your twenties that way is that you want to be as successful as possible as young as possible. Let me try to persuade you to rethink that.

I entered college in the year John F. Kennedy was inaugurated. I recall envying Ted Sorenson, JFK's chief speechwriter and one of his closest advisors, who was just thirty-two years old. JFK himself was just forty-three years old. His attorney general, brother Robert, was just thirty-five. All this combined to make me think of my career trajectory in wildly unrealistic terms. I was supposed to be a rising figure by my late twenties, blossoming in my thirties, and reaching the apex of my career by my early forties. My fifties and sixties? Would I even be alive by then? They were so far in the misty future that they were not part of my personal timeline.

It was a completely understandable way of looking at time. On your twenty-second birthday, as many years separate you from forty as separate you from your fourth birthday party. The years from twenty-two to forty seem like a lifetime of their own. And you, like me, have role models of spectacular achievement at a young age—Mark Zuckerberg, for example, and the other *wunderkinder* of the IT revolution. There are always a few people in the fields we are entering who deform our sense of how our careers should unfold. But not only are they anomalous; many are object lessons in the downsides of early success.

The first reason to be wary of early success is the concept and the reality of apprenticeship. It takes a long time to become expert in almost any of the crafts that go into making successful careers. Much empirical work has been done on the subject. The most famous is Herbert Simon's calculation that to become an expert requires mastering enough "chunks" of material relevant to your field. The number of chunks is usually described as fifty thousand, mastery of which usually requires at least ten years. So whatever you set out to become good at—being a manager, arguing legal cases, covering news stories, analyzing social science data, or making smart investment decisions—you will start out producing imperfect results. Even the prodigies are not immune to the need for apprenticeships. Steve Jobs made Apple a great start-up story when he was in his twenties, but he also committed amateurish mistakes and was ousted when he was thirty. By the time he returned to Apple in his forties, he was a brilliant CEO.

That Steve Jobs did so much better in his forties points to the second reason why you should be wary of early success. The development of a certain kind of mature judgment is hard to rush. The Greeks called it *phronesis*, usually translated as *practical wisdom* (the concept will reappear in tip #27). An essential part of *phronesis* is not just the acquisition of chunks of knowledge, but life experience.

Social scientists have explored the ages at which famous people have accomplished their greatest work and thereby demonstrated that life experience isn't always important. In sports, chess, and pure mathematics, for example, the greatest achievements usually occur in the twenties and early thirties. Raw physical and cognitive gifts are what's needed, plus intense work. Life experience is peripheral. Nor does life experience necessarily play a large part in musical composition or the visual arts. Many composers and painters have done great work in their twenties and thirties. But even in those fields, life experience can bring additional depth to their creations. The median age for artists' and composers' greatest work is forty, which means that half of the greatest work occurred after forty. In literature, life experience is a crucial part of the great writer's toolkit, and, accordingly, the median age at which the greatest works have been written is around fifty.

Your career is likely to bear more resemblance to that of a writer than that of an athlete or painter. You should look ahead to your forties as the time when you will be at your peak of creativity, technical proficiency, and energy, and also have enough *phronesis* to realize your potential. The more your field depends on good judgment that comes only from experience, the longer you can expect to sustain a high level of performance into your fifties and sixties. To put it another way: Even if you wait as late as thirty to start accumulating the fifty thousand chunks of expertise, you will still have completed that apprenticeship when you approach the peak of your other powers in your forties.

So push out your time horizon and don't get frustrated if what you hoped would be a meteoric rise proves to be more measured. You're not failing; you're getting better at your craft and can reasonably aspire to master it one day. In the meantime, consult Wikipedia to check on the lives of those who became conspicuously successful at a young age. Ted Sorenson? After JFK was assassinated, he had a financially successful career as an attorney and remained a participant in politics, but, like sports heroes, rock stars, and pure mathematicians, he had to turn forty knowing that his most exciting professional years were behind him. How sad. And how happy you should be that you aren't going to be a famous presidential aide at thirty-two.

22. Get real jobs.

Let's get down to specifics. Just how are you supposed to go about enhancing your twenties?

Many of you may skip this tip. You've grown up in a middle-class or working-class neighborhood in a big city, in a small city or town, or on a farm. You've been working at all kinds of jobs since your midteens, and you've gone to school with students from all kinds of backgrounds. For you, there's nothing broken that this tip fixes. It is intended for a particular subset of readers, to wit:

You have grown up in an upper-middle-class household in a metropolitan area, attended good K–12 schools with other children of the upper middle class, and attended a selective college. Insofar as this description applies to you, you have lived in substantial isolation from mainstream America. You may not realize it, but if you were to be inserted into an ordinary middle-class or working-class community to live for a few months, you would feel like a foreigner. Have you ever seen one of those movies in which a clueless city slicker is thrown into a small town in the West or South? You would be playing the leading role.

Getting to Know the Middle

If you've grown up in the upper-middle-class bubble, you may well have had contact with the most disadvantaged elements of American society. Many upper-middle-class parents make sure their teenage children volunteer once a week at the local soup kitchen or spend a week working for Habitat for Humanity in the summer. Sometimes the parents are motivated by a sincere desire to strengthen their child's sense of social responsibility; sometimes by a sincere desire to strengthen their child's application to an elite college. Either way, such experiences are good. I hope you've had some. But they can produce a false sense of knowledge. Working at a soup kitchen once a week may have exposed you to some of America's most problem-ridden communities. But you've still never been exposed to the vast middle: the majority of American communities that are neither affluent nor in poverty, but function just fine—and in ways that you should understand.

So you need to think about ways of breaking out of the upper-middle-class bubble. The subsequent two tips will help if you have already graduated from college. This one will help if you're still in school: You can find a summer job that is not an internship.

Internships are affirmative action for the advantaged. Who can afford to spend the summer without making any money? Students whose parents are subsidizing them. Who are you going to be around if you get an internship? In most cases, other upper-middle-class college students just like you and upper-middle-class supervisors just like your parents.

Furthermore, the value of internships is ridiculously oversold. Let's be serious. The chances that your summer of interning at AEI or your congressperson's office or the Museum of Modern Art is going to help you network your way into a terrific job are slim. It's just as likely to produce an "opportunity" that seduces you into a job after college that you don't really like that much, just because you have a connection. But neither of those outcomes is likely. The typical internship may well be pleasant, but it's not life-changing, and it doesn't send you back to school with nifty new job skills. You will have simply spent a summer hanging out with the same kinds of people you've always known in a generically familiar environment.

Finding a summer job that isn't an internship is easier than you might think, even in a bad job market. There are lots of summer jobs available for college students at vacation resorts—not at the high-end places like Aspen that are open year-round and have professional staffs, but at the fishing resorts, dude ranches, restaurants, and bars that open only for the summer and have to re-staff every year. The Mountain West is a rich source of such jobs; so are the summer vacation areas of Minnesota, Wisconsin, Michigan, the Ozarks, the Great Smoky Mountains, the Adirondacks, and northern New England. Almost all of those jobs are filled by application during the winter months, and one of your options is to think ahead and apply for one. But you can still find a job even if you haven't thought ahead. Just show up at a resort area in early June after the accepted college applicants were supposed to have arrived. Some of them will be no-shows (college students are unreliable), and employers will be looking for replacements.

What's so great about waiting tables in Montana or helping children bait hooks in Minnesota? Partly, they're the jobs that are available. Ordinary jobs are hard to get for just three months, because employers know you're not going to stay. But jobs at summer resorts also have a specific advantage: They are service jobs. Many of you have been waited upon constantly until this point in your life and you will be waited upon constantly as a successful adult. It is essential that you know what it's like to do the waiting upon. Once you have been a server in a restaurant, you will never again look at dining in a restaurant as you did before you were a server. If you have ever had to attend to customers in a busy store, you are less likely to be an obnoxious customer thereafter.

Working in a service job at an ordinary resort, store,

or restaurant will also bring you into direct contact with all sorts of people you would have never encountered as equals in your upper-middle-class bubble. Some of them will become friends, and you will be inoculated against condescension in the future. Others you won't care for—jerks are part of every social class—but at least you will have concrete reasons for not caring for them. One of my daughters went to a high school where some of the other students were self-described rednecks. She didn't share many interests with them, and they weren't her best friends. But she also knew them as flesh-and-blood people. When she went off to an elite college, it made her angry to hear her fellow students refer sneeringly to rednecks. They didn't have the right to use that word, she told them, because they didn't know what they were talking about. That's the point. We aren't required to love all of our fellow Americans. But we should know from personal experience what we're talking about.

23. Confront your inner hothouse flower.

The options in this tip are good ideas for many reasons, but they are especially important for a subset of readers: those of you who have had parents and teachers who were too caring and wonderful for your own good. Mom and Dad listened to you and rarely punished you, and even then only mildly and for appropriate reasons. They praised you when you did well, consoled you when you didn't, and were otherwise patient and understanding. Your teachers were fair, encouraging, and patient and understanding. You cannot remember a time since you were ten when an adult other than Mom or Dad raised his voice to you, because every important adult in your life has been patient and understanding.

This tip is for you, because you have had a deprived childhood. I'm not talking about your family's socio-economic status (it might be anything) but about your excessively placid childhood. You probably possess two of the most important personal qualities for success—high cognitive ability and good interpersonal skills. But it is unlikely that you have already developed another important trait: resilience.

The first dictionary definition of *resilience* is "the physical property of a material that can return to its original shape or position after deformation that does not exceed its elastic limit." In humans, "elastic limit" is variable. When exercised, it increases. You've had no exercise. You're approaching adulthood with the elastic limit of a Baccarat champagne flute.

It's not your fault. It's not a character flaw. You may have the potential elastic limit of a SuperBall, but if

you've grown up in a loving and untroubled environment, that potential is unrealized. Here's the problem:
You can be sure that your resilience will be tested sooner
or later. When it happens, you don't want to shatter into
glittering shards. If my description fits you, now is the
time, when you're still single and more or less without
responsibilities, to start exercising your elastic limit.

Two generic strategies are open to you. The first is to
enlist in one of the branches of America's armed forces.
I'm serious. I know it's at least two years of active duty,
and that sounds like an eternity; I know that going into
the armed forces doesn't fit into the career plans of
most of my readers. But you can be sure that when you
come out of those years in uniform, your elastic limit
will have moved far closer to the SuperBall end of the
spectrum.

If you're on a university campus, just look around
at the students who have come to college after a stint
in the military. Compare their maturity and focus to
their fellow students of the same age who haven't had
that experience. For that matter, compare their maturity and focus to your own. They have had to deal with
supervisor-subordinate relationships of a kind that no
civilian job matches. They have been required to perform under conditions more stressful than you'll find
in almost any civilian job and in situations where the

penalties for mistakes can be far greater than in almost any civilian job. They have had to deal with all kinds of people, from every socioeconomic, ethnic, and educational background. I will add as full disclosure that one of my own few persistent regrets is that I did not have those experiences. There is, however, one gigantic caveat: If you join the armed forces, you may have to go to war. You must have decided beforehand that you are prepared to do so.

The other generic strategy is to pick a place in a strange part of the world that you'd like to get to know (London and Paris don't count as strange), buy a one-way airplane ticket, and go. Get off the plane, find a job, any job, learn the language, don't live exclusively among ex-pats, and stay for at least three years (less than three has the psychology of an extended visit, not a life abroad). In my case, I joined the Peace Corps, went to Thailand, and ended up staying for five years before I came back to America to go to graduate school.

The ideal outcome is that you become at home in an alien culture. It's hard to describe how satisfying it is. It's like having backstage privileges at some grand event. There you are, in Istanbul or Addis Ababa or Bangkok, watching the tourists studying their tourist maps and clumsily bargaining with taxi drivers, while you, now the insider, speak the language and have come (after false starts) to understand the more subtle and difficult language of social cues. That kind of achievement is also as close to something that is entirely your own doing as anything you will ever accomplish in life. It hasn't flowed naturally from your upbringing or your education. You will have thrown yourself into a situation where you were completely incompetent and made yourself competent—not competent at a few discrete skills, but competent at living in a different world. The self-confidence this produces and the satisfaction of having done it stays with you for the rest of your life.

There are options besides the armed forces or the one-way ticket abroad. But just moving out of your parents' home and taking a job in an unfamiliar American city is unlikely to do the trick if your new setting is filled with people like you. Backpacking for a year, staying at the same places where all the other backpackers stay, is unlikely to do the trick either. You've got to spend serious time coping with situations that stress you psychologically and with people from alien backgrounds who stretch your understanding of life. Better to exercise your elastic limit now, when the penalties for errors are low, instead of fifteen years from now, when lack of experience in coping with adversity could be catastrophic.

24. Think about what kinds of itches need scratching.

Two accomplishments will, if you pull them off, almost surely produce happiness: Find work that you enjoy, and find your soul mate. Let's start with the easy part: finding your vocation.

A few of you already know what that vocation is. You have fallen in love with medicine or the violin or flying airplanes, and you want nothing more than to spend the rest of your life doing those things. It hasn't been a rational, deliberate decision, but a response to an overpowering sense of "this is what I was put on earth to do." Good for you. If you want to go directly from college to medical school, Juilliard, or flight training, you'll get no argument from me. The rest of you—an extremely large majority, I bet—have an urgently important task ahead.

The first step is to realize that you probably have a surprisingly narrow set of high-prestige options in mind: one of the classic professions such as medicine, law, engineering, or academia, or a career in finance, corporate management, or public administration.

If you aren't careful, that kind of tunnel vision about career possibilities is going to keep you from identifying all sorts of ways of making a living that are more fun. Instead of trying to choose among specific careers, think first about the things you especially enjoy. Here are some possibilities:

- You enjoy being outdoors.
- You enjoy solving puzzles.
- You enjoy interacting with new people, getting them to reveal what makes them tick.
- You enjoy solitude, figuring things out all by yourself.
- You enjoy being part of contests that end in victory or defeat.
- You enjoy security and predictability.
- You enjoy risk.
- You enjoy being in places where most people don't get to go—backstage, inside the yellow tape of a crime scene, in the locker room, in the situation room.
- You enjoy being onstage, in the spotlight, the center of attention.
- You enjoy closure: finishing a thing and moving on to something new.
- You enjoy open-ended tasks, or creating things that are large and complicated.

Once you have identified what things you instinctively enjoy, *then* start thinking about a career.

Let's suppose that two of your itches that need scratching are interacting with new people and figuring out what makes them tick. In that case, one possibility is a conventional educational career (such as a Ph.D. in psychology) leading to a conventional profession (for example, clinical psychology). But suppose that you also love taking risks and being part of contests that end in victory or defeat. You need a job that scratches those itches too. Why not think about a job that involves selling things? You will spend every working day engaged in a variety of contests, there's some risk involved too, and you will most definitely be interacting with new people and figuring out what makes them tick.

Going into sales is not exactly what your parents had in mind for you? Not prestigious enough? Here's where the constrictions of your socialization may come into play. When you saw the word *sales* you probably had an image of someone selling cosmetics, cars, or houses. But exotic things require salespeople too. Yachts. Antiquities. Weapons systems. Things that will put you in settings more interesting than a psychologist's office and around people who are more interesting than other psychologists.

That's just one example. Given any set of things that scratch your itches, you can replicate the exercise: Start with the obvious career, and then step back and explore alternatives that weren't visible until you took off your blinders and reacquired peripheral vision. You don't have to figure it all out on your own. Go online, search on "aptitude tests," and you will find many resources to help you identify your itches. Pull up lists of occupations. You'll be startled by how many interesting ones haven't been on your radar screen.

You have no idiosyncratic itches that you enjoy scratching? Then heading off to a graduate program right after college is not the right choice. You haven't the least idea whether you're headed into a career you will enjoy.

25. Being judgmental is good, and you don't have a choice anyway.

So you've gotten out of your protective bubble, if you were ever in one, you've acquired resilience even if you had a happy childhood, and you've given yourself a chance to discover a career that you will really enjoy. In today's culture, you've still got a few more issues to think about, because today's universities have done more than abandon their role in teaching you to love rigor. They have also abandoned their traditional function of requiring you to think about what it means to live a good life.

I had better take a moment to make sure we're on the same page. What I am about to say assumes that the purpose of a human life is not just to pass the time between birth and death as pleasantly as possible, with as little trouble as possible. Life should consist of something more than leisure and transient pleasures. Can we agree on that?

If so, then let's take the next step: A life well lived has transcendent value, whether that transcendence is defined in religious or secular terms. Putting aside specific doctrinal differences, a core aspect of the Western view of transcendence, whether Judeo-Christian or Aristotelian, is that there are excellences associated with the state of being human. Living a good life means realizing those excellences in our lives as best we can. Put another way, we are under a moral obligation to do our best to realize the best that human beings can be. To neglect that obligation is to waste our lives. Can we also broadly agree on that?

For those who are still with me, the first step in thinking about what it means to live a good life is to accept that you're going to have to make judgments—not just statements about your own tastes and preferences, but judgments about what are the excellences that human beings should strive to realize, which in turn means judgments about what is right and wrong, good and evil.

Of the many pernicious aspects of today's academic culture, I think the worst is its celebration of nonjudgmentalism. I assume you've heard it many times (I certainly have) when you think you've made an incisive argument: "You're being judgmental." It's a glib, contemptible response. The ability to make judgments is what distinguishes *Homo sapiens* from every other living creature. But the ability to make judgments carries with it the obligation to do so. You don't have a choice.

Defining *Judgmental*

The negative connotations of *judgmental*—harsh, arbitrary, condemnatory moral judgments—have taken over so completely that I can't recall the last time I heard *judgmental* used in a neutral sense. But historically (and still in some dictionaries), the first meaning of *judgmental* was simply "of, relating to, or involving judgment." That's the way I'm using it here.

Let's start with the distinction between personal taste and judgment, choosing a noninflammatory example to make the point. You and a friend are standing in front of two paintings. One is Titian's *Venus of Urbino* (Google it if you aren't familiar with it) and the other is a painting of a nude on black velvet. You ask your friend which painting he prefers. He says he prefers the one on black velvet. You have no basis for arguing with him. He likes it better, in the same way that he may like Dr Pepper better than Coke. *De gustibus non est disputandum.*

But suppose instead that you ask him which is the artistically superior painting, and he says, "You can't say one painting is better than another. It's just a matter of opinion." He's wrong. Now we're not talking about taste alone, but about a body of knowledge regarding the aesthetics of representational art. It is true of all sorts of topics about which people have different tastes, but which also involve knowledge—painting, music, fiction, wine, gardens, architecture. People who know a lot about these subjects have reasons for comparing different examples and rendering judgments that one is a better realization of some underlying measures of excellence than another one is.

This holds true independently of taste. If you know a lot about wine, for example, it may be that your own personal taste runs to big, fruit-driven wines. But that doesn't prevent you judging that a delicate French Burgundy is a better realization of its type than another that "tastes better" according to your personal preferences. An element of expert judgment in these fields exists independently of personal preferences. Thus everyone who is an expert on representational art will unhesitatingly say that *Venus of Urbino* is superior to the nude on black velvet, and you will be powerless to argue with them. If you object to that assertion, go to YouTube, search on *Venus of Urbino*, and watch some of the videos. People who know a lot about art can look at *Venus of Urbino* for a long time and the looking alone can absorb their full attention. There's a lot to see and talk about. Those knowledgeable people cannot be similarly absorbed by looking at the nude painted on black velvet. They can talk about its social context. They can talk about the meaning of the female nude in the construction of gender. But there's not much to get out of the looking. Yes, they are being judgmental about the relative aesthetic merits of the two paintings. But that judgment is based on the power of the human mind to make meaningful discriminations.

Now go back to the reaction of your companion: "You can't say one painting is better than another. It's just a matter of opinion." He is not really being non-judgmental. If he refuses to accept that there are any objective differences, expressible as continua from positive to negative, between *Venus of Urbino* and the nude painted on black velvet, he is not standing above the fray. He has just made a judgment on a grand scale about the capacity of the human mind to assess information.

Nor does he have the option of saying that differences exist but that he will not judge them. To notice a difference is to have an opinion about it—unless one refuses to think. And that is my ultimate objection to nonjudgmentalism. We can refuse to voice our judgments, but we cannot keep from having them unless we refuse to think about what is before our eyes.

Why did I go on at such length about the *Venus of Urbino*? Because it let me put my argument on the table without all the passions that are aroused as soon as I turn to more important realms. Suppose that instead of art, you and your friend are talking about marriage versus cohabitation, and your friend says, "Marriage isn't for me." That is a statement of his tastes and preferences and not open to argument. If he says instead, "Marriage works for some people, not for others; it's no big deal what people choose," then my point about artistic merit is unchanged, except more emphatic: *You mustn't indulge yourself in that kind of flaccid nonjudgmental nonsense.* Marriage has historically been the central organizing institution of society and the framework for socializing children, but it has also been undergoing radical changes in recent decades. Its proper role in today's culture is as momentous as issues get. To say something like, "Marriage works for some people, not for others; it's no big deal what people choose," is as idiotic as saying that it's a matter of opinion whether a Titian painting is superior to artistic dreck, except that in this instance there is a moral dimension to your obligation to think through your judgments that doesn't burden your judgments about art.

I want to emphasize that being judgmental is not the same as being intolerant. It is appropriate to be tolerant of behaviors that you wouldn't engage in yourself, and even ones of which you disapprove but which you also judge to fall within the range of choices that people should be entitled to make in a free society. But you can't let your desire to be tolerant get in the way of your obligation to reach moral judgments. You need to think through your assessment of alternative codes of behavior, drawing upon as much accumulated human wisdom as you can about virtue and vice, and about the consequences of different behaviors for human flourishing. You not only need to do it; you must. The failure to do so doesn't define you as nonjudgmental. It defines you as lazy. To refuse to think about what constitutes moral behavior—not just for you, but for human beings as a species—is to reject one of the fundamental responsibilities of living a human life. Which leads to the next tip:

26. Come to grips with the distinction between *can do* and *may do*.

Case #1. A stand-up comic has an act that consists entirely of scatological jokes. He has great comedic talent and always keeps his large audiences in stitches. In conversation with others, would you be willing to use the word *vulgar* to describe his act?

Case #2. An incoming CEO negotiates an employment contract with the board of directors that guarantees him a severance package worth $30 million when he leaves the company. He turns out to be a terrible CEO, bringing the company to the brink of bankruptcy by the time the board fires him, but he takes the $30 million owed to him under the terms of the contract. Would you be willing to use the word *unseemly* to describe his acceptance of the money?

Case #3. An investment advisor has a client who is attracted to flashy but unsound investments. To please the client and keep his substantial fees flowing, the investment advisor recommends investments he knows will please his client, not the ones he believes to be the best ones. Would you be willing to use the word *dishonorable* to describe the advisor's behavior?

Probably you would not personally choose to emulate the stand-up comedian, the CEO, or the investment advisor. But a vague sense of "I wouldn't do that myself" is not what I'm interested in. Rather, I wonder whether you subscribe to a coherent code of behavior that leads you to be willing to characterize those behaviors—all of which are legal—with the words *vulgar, unseemly,* or *dishonorable.*

I deliberately chose words that are unfashionable. We're willing to say that someone's behavior is "inappropriate," but the words *vulgar, unseemly,* and *dishonorable* all have a hard edge to them, conveying an element of contempt as well as disapproval. I'm in favor of bringing them back.

Traditionally, people subscribed to codes of behavior that were unenforceable by the law, and they judged one another according to their allegiance to those codes of behavior. Now, the opposite is true. Our era does still have some commandments in force. Thou shalt not make racist, sexist, or homophobic remarks. Thou shalt not make judgmental remarks about the lifestyles or values of others. But we have turned the traditional understanding upside down. Instead of undertaking to judge ourselves and others according to our allegiance to an unwritten code of social behavior, we promise to *abstain* from judging others and consider ourselves aggrieved if others judge us.

In the previous tip about judgmentalism, I was talking about the ways in which judgment is more than just a matter of opinion and about the necessity of judging—we have no choice, because even the refusal to judge is a commitment to a point of view. Now, I'm asking you to look inward and ask yourself whether you've thought through the implications of the distinction between *can do* and *may do*.

I am a libertarian, and as such I believe that people should have the legal freedom to do almost anything that doesn't involve force or fraud. I am also an admirer of both Edmund Burke and Adam Smith, and as such believe there are many things that people *can* do but *may not* do—that is, do not have the freedom to do without reproach. An eminent English judge a century ago, John Fletcher Moulton, put it nicely: "Between 'can do' and 'may do' ought to exist the whole realm which recognizes the sway of duty, fairness, sympathy, taste, and all the other things that make life beautiful and society possible." He called this realm "obedience to the unenforceable," and it is the passing of that realm that has led to the disuse of *vulgar, unseemly,* and *dishonorable.*

By asking you to contemplate what made you uneasy in my three examples, I am hoping to awaken your inner judgmentalism. I hope that you will decide that *vulgar, unseemly,* and *dishonorable* apply to certain kinds of behavior, and will feel free to let your opinion about such behavior be known. For those of you who don't see anything troubling with the behavior of the stand-up comedian, the CEO, or the investment advisor, my question is, can you think of any behaviors at all that people *can* do but *may not* do? If the answer is yes, I would be curious to know why those behaviors qualify when my examples did not. If the answer is no, then I will render a judgment of my own: You belong to the category of people who are contributing to the deterioration of civic life.

27. Come to grips with the difference between being nice and being good.

Just as the words *vulgar, unseemly,* and *dishonorable* are not ordinarily used in conversation today, neither is *virtue.* The disuse of *virtue* is part of today's nonjudgmentalism. It's acceptable for people to have *values,* which will differ across people (and who is to say that one set of values is better than another?), but the word *virtue* carries with it connotations of invariance and objectivity. And rightly so. Let me make a brief case for the objective, universal applicability of the cardinal virtues in our quest to become not just nice, but good.

Nice and *good* are different. Being nice involves immediate actions and immediate consequences—you give water to the thirsty and comfort to the afflicted right here, right now. Being good involves living in the world so that you contribute to the welfare of your fellow human beings. Sometimes the immediate and long-term consequences are consistent with being nice; sometimes they are in conflict. That's where the importance of the cardinal virtues comes in.

The four cardinal virtues were originated by the Greeks. They subsequently got their label from the Latin *cardo*, meaning "hinge," because they are pivotal: All the other virtues, and the living of a virtuous life, depend on them. If you took an introductory philosophy course in college, they were probably translated from the Greek as *courage, justice, temperance*, and *prudence*.

Courage, meaning not just physical but also moral courage, is pivotal because no virtue is sustained in the face of adversity without it.

Justice—as defined by Aristotle, giving everyone his rightful due—is pivotal because it is a precondition for behaving in other virtuous ways (for example, the virtue of compassion rightly takes different forms for people in different circumstances).

Temperance is, to modern ears, an unfortunate label. It sounds insipid. Aren't we supposed to live life to the fullest? Haven't we decided, along with Mae West and Liberace, that too much of a good thing can be wonderful? But when you stop to think about it, too much of a good thing isn't wonderful. It cloys. Satiates. The pleasure ends. If you still are unhappy with the idea of being temperate, think in terms of self-restraint and knowing oneself, both of which are part of the meaning of *sophro-syne,* the word Plato used for this virtue. Temperance is pivotal because, without it, any subsidiary virtue will be ignored when it competes with natural appetites.

That leaves *prudence,* the cardinal virtue that requires the most work and time for you to acquire. It is also the virtue with the most unappealing label of all, with its connotation of timidity. The idea of other people saying of me, "Charles is very prudent," is mortifying. But this is a function of evolving language. *Prudence* has acquired negative connotations that it did not formerly possess. Let's go back to the original Greek word for this cardinal virtue, *phronesis,* which I introduced in tip #21.

Aristotle talks about two kinds of wisdom. One is the ability to apprehend reality and make the pieces fit together—roughly, the kind of wisdom that underlies science. *Phronesis* is the word Aristotle used for the other kind of wisdom, better translated in the twenty-first century as *practical wisdom. Phronesis* is harder to come by than scientific knowledge. Studying reality is not enough. Practical wisdom means the ability to rightly assess the consequences of a course of action. Knowledge is necessary, but so is experience. You might want to be compassionate, for example, but without practical wisdom you might behave in ways that cause suffering rather than relieve it. Balancing all the considerations that go into rightly assessing long-term consequences is difficult, and it requires both thoughtfulness and a deep understanding of human life. Thus the cardinal virtue of practical wisdom is pivotal because it is the precondition for behaving in other virtuous ways.

Hence my proposition: The cardinal virtues are indispensable to being good. I don't mean that theoretically, but in the course of going about your daily life. You really, truly, *must* be courageous, just, temperate, and possess practical wisdom if you also wish to be dependably kind, merciful, compassionate, tolerant, patient, or to practice any of the other virtues. Lacking the cardinal virtues, you can act in those other virtuous ways haphazardly, and occasionally have the effect you wish, but you cannot consistently have the effect you wish, nor will you be able to bring yourself to behave in those other virtuous ways when the going gets tough. You will still mean well. You will still be nice. You won't be good.

You don't need to be an Aristotelian to be good. For two millennia, the world's other most influential ethical system was Confucianism. The central virtue in Confucianism is *ren*, the summation of all subsidiary virtues. *Ren* translates as humaneness or benevolence, but the Confucian conception of *ren* is richer than either word conveys. *Ren* incorporates the idea of reciprocity (a form of the Golden Rule), which overlaps with Aristotle's concept of justice. *Ren* incorporates courage. Confucianism is emphatic about the need for temperance and self-control. And one of the chief components of *ren* is the considered, accurate appraisal of consequences that Aristotle described as practical wisdom. If you are a good Confucian, you will be practicing the cardinal virtues.

Whether you find inspiration in the Western or the Eastern tradition is a minor issue. What is unacceptable is to go through life thinking that being nice is enough. You must come to grips with the requirements for being good.

28. Don't ruin your love affair with yourself.

Aristotle and Confucius shared another crucial insight: Virtue consists of learned behaviors that become habits, in the same way that physical fitness results from the habit of exercise. You aren't fit because you learn the physiological requirements of fitness and spend a frenzied week at the gym a couple of times a year. Similarly, you aren't generous because you write a big check to United Way a couple of times a year.

How do you acquire the habits of virtue, so that virtuous behavior is reflexive? Let's take a prosaic example that has happened to all of us in some form. You've left the supermarket and realize that the checkout person gave you $20 too much change. You're already halfway to the car with your arms full of groceries. The mistake is not your fault. Let's assume you know that the checkout clerk won't have to pay for it. It's a huge supermarket chain making millions in profits. Do you schlep all the way back to the store to give the money back?

A convenient resource in making the right decision is to take great enjoyment in a self-conscious image of yourself—in this instance, to take great enjoyment in thinking of yourself as incorruptibly honest. What happens if you don't return the $20? You ruin your love affair with yourself. You don't need to be self-righteous to make this strategy work. I assume that I have a price at which I would be willing to ruin my love affair with myself. I don't know what it is. But I am quite sure that it is more than $20.

The same kind of thinking—"Is it worth ruining my love affair with myself?"—applies to many virtues. Probably you like to think of yourself as a generous person. Protect the pleasure of that self-image by always rounding up. If three of you have gone to lunch together and the check plus tip comes to $114.66, don't divide by 3 and count out $38.22. Drop $40 on the table, and let the extra augment the tip. Speaking of tipping, always lean toward overtipping, and overtip lavishly if the service has been unusually good. If you're bargaining over a price, keep the context in mind. When a guy you know is going to paint your house, pay his asking price. Love thinking of yourself as a generous person, and you will find that protecting your self-image will automatically cultivate the habit of generosity, occasionally including big checks that are not necessarily tax deductible.

The list could go on. Each day brings choices that in small ways enable you to continue your love affair with yourself or damage it. If you think in these terms, you will be surprised how many day-to-day moral decisions become easy and reflexive. Humility (see tip #11) is still one of the virtues you should cultivate. But vanity has its uses.

ON THE PURSUIT OF HAPPINESS

Happiness is a simple concept. Philosophically, the Western understanding comes from Aristotle, whose discussion of happiness in the *Nicomachean Ethics* is complete and persuasive. Skipping a lot of nuances, the definition of happiness that comes out of that tradition is *lasting and justified satisfaction with life as a whole.* The two key words in that sentence are *lasting*, specifying that the satisfactions cannot consist of ephemeral pleasures, and *justified*, meaning that it is not enough that one have, for example, a drug-induced sense of satisfaction. The separate satisfactions that go into overall satisfaction must be grounded in reality. They must also be in accord with virtue. The sadist may claim that he has lasting and justified satisfaction from a lifetime of inflicting pain on other people, but we are not obliged to accept his claim as legitimate.

In ordinary life, lasting and justified satisfactions arise from only a few sources. I argue that they come from just four: family, vocation (which includes passionately pursued avocations and causes), community, and faith. If that sounds too dogmatic, try to think of a source of lasting and justified satisfactions that *doesn't* fit into one of those four domains. It's hard.

It is not necessary for you to tap all four of these domains to be happy. There are happy atheists and happy single people. But the more of the four you are engaged in, the better your odds are.

29. Show up.

"Eighty percent of success is showing up," Woody Allen famously said, and the same applies to happiness. *Showing up* means giving yourself the possibility of finding satisfaction in the four domains, not necessarily succeeding.

Not showing up for family means deciding not to marry, or deliberately choosing to get into extended relationships only with people who are unavailable for marriage, or fleeing whenever a relationship starts to become dangerously important, or marrying and then putting no effort into it.

Not showing up for vocation means deliberately choosing an occupation that you know will make you a lot of money (e.g., finance) or job security (e.g., academia) even though you know that you aren't absorbed by the work.

Not showing up for community means choosing to live in anonymous apartment complexes in a city, or in affluent but impersonal suburbs, or deliberately staying aloof from your neighbors in a real community.

Not showing up for faith means never bothering to take an interest in religion.

A Word About "Not Showing Up for Family"

My use of marriage as an essential part of showing up for family raises obvious questions. What about gay and lesbian couples? What about families consisting of a never-married parent with children? What about unmarried adults who remain close to their parents, siblings, aunts, uncles, cousins, nieces, and nephews? All of these situations are ones in which people did not "show up for family" in the formulation I used, and yet they can and do get deep and lasting satisfaction from family.

My answer is that I was unable to devise an economical statement of what constitutes "not showing up for family" without using marriage, especially now that gay marriage is legal in many states and will soon be legal in many more. A formulation like "not making yourself emotionally available for long-term loving commitments to other human beings" doesn't cut it for me (I'm a curmudgeon, remember). For ninety-odd percent of the population, showing up for family means making oneself available for marriage.

Just by showing up, the likelihood that you will fall into deep engagement in one or more of the four domains increases enormously, and so does the likelihood that you will reach old age with deep satisfactions about who you have been and what you have done.

The problem you face is that it has become so easy to avoid showing up. It is something genuinely new under the sun, with its origins in the last quarter of the nineteenth century. Consider: If it is the year 1875 and you are anyone except a wealthy person living in one of a handful of large cities, what are your choices about how to spend your day? Almost nothing in your daily life does *not* involve engagement with family, vocation, community, or faith. Even the things you do purely for fun almost inevitably involve family or friends: If you want to listen to music, you and family or friends will have to sing or play music yourselves. If you want to play a game, it will have to be with family or friends. Being a passive spectator at the theater, an athletic event, or a public concert is so rare that each occasion stands out in your memory.

What was true in 1875 had been true throughout human history. Day to day, people didn't have any choice but to show up. Then the phonograph and motion pictures were invented, providing the first opportunity for people to have entertainment besides books provided for them by impersonal means on a daily basis, but those by themselves had trivial effects on life as a whole. A half century later, the spread of commercial radio radically expanded the ways in which life could be brought to people on a platter and the ease with which it could be done. The spread of commercial television in the late 1940s pushed the process still further. But those distractions from the four domains were as nothing compared to the ways in which the IT revolution has made it possible for us to occupy ourselves all day long and all night long by sitting alone in front of a screen.

You are not going to reach old age satisfied with who you have been and what you have done because you interfaced with a screen. Thus the first essential step in the pursuit of happiness: Show up.

30. Take the clichés about fame and fortune seriously.

One of my assumptions about you is that you are ambitious, meaning that you have private dreams of becoming famous, rich, or both, and intend to devote intense energy over the next few decades in the pursuit of those dreams. That's as it should be. I look with suspicion on any talented twenty-something who doesn't feel at least a little bit that way.

Furthermore, I am not one to despise the rewards of riches. I have loved flying on private jets, the few times I have had the opportunity, and I have a taste for first-growth Bordeaux that I wish I could afford to indulge more often. I'm not so sure about fame. I am occasionally recognized when I am among people who read books on social policy (not a big part of the population), and it's mildly gratifying, but I would think that true fame—being recognized whenever you walk down the street or enter a restaurant—would get real old real fast. But so many entertainers and politicians seem addicted to fame that I would probably be seduced too if the chance came my way.

In any case, I'm not discouraging you from going for the big bucks and the spotlight. I wish you luck. But suppose you arrive at age forty and you enjoy your work, have found your soul mate, and are raising a couple of terrific kids, but must recognize that you will probably never become either rich or famous. At that point, it's important to supplement your youthful ambition with mature understanding. That's where the clichés come in—the ones about money not buying happiness and fame being empty. The problem is to feel the truth of those clichés, not just agree with them intellectually. I hereby offer two pieces of testimony that struck me forcefully.

"Money can't buy happiness" is such a cliché that the words go through our heads without stopping. Just a slight variation made me understand. Many years ago, I was watching a television profile of David Geffen, the billionaire music and film producer. At some point in the interview, Geffen said, "Show me someone who thinks that money buys happiness, and I'll show you someone who has never had a lot of money." It was the same thought as "money can't buy happiness," but with a twist, accompanied by an ineffably sad smile on Geffen's face that said he had been there, done that, and knew what he was talking about. My visceral recognition was reinforced by one of the shots during the profile, taken from the front of Geffen's Gulfstream down the length of the plane, along the rows of empty leather seats and sofas, to Geffen sitting all alone in the rear.

Author and *New York Times* columnist David Brooks is responsible for the second testimony that spoke to me powerfully. In his book *The Social Animal*, Brooks created two fictional characters, Harold and Erica, as a framework for his narrative. He gave Erica an enviable career as a CEO, presidential advisor, and cabinet secretary. Brooks says this about her at the end of her career:

> [Erica] was treated as a significant person wherever she went. Strangers would approach and say they were honored to meet her. This didn't make her feel happy by itself, but it did mean that she was no longer gnawed by the sort of ambition anxiety that had driven her through much of her life. Recognition and wealth, she had learned, do not produce happiness, but they do liberate you from the worries that plague people who lack but desire those things.

Read that passage again, slowly. It is precisely correct. An unavoidable side effect of ambition is to be gnawed by ambition anxiety about whether you're going to succeed. You're bound to feel it in your twenties and thirties. Put it away in your forties. By that time, you should have learned enough to recognize that fame and wealth are trivial—really, truly *trivial*—to a life well lived.

31. Take religion seriously, especially if you've been socialized not to.

Don't bother to read this one if you're already satisfyingly engaged in a religious tradition.

Now that we're alone, here's where a lot of you stand when it comes to religion: It's not for you. You don't mind if other people are devout, but you don't get it. Smart people don't believe that stuff anymore.

Perhaps you are explicitly an atheist. Even if you are an agnostic, you don't spend much time worrying about God, because there's no point. If a God exists, it cannot be the kind of God who has anything to do with this flyspeck world, let alone with the lives of the individual human beings on it.

I can be sure that's what many of you think because your generation of high-IQ college-attending young people, like mine fifty years ago, has been as thoroughly socialized to be secular as our counterparts in preceding generations were socialized to be devout. Some of you grew up with parents who were not religious, and you've never given religion a thought. Others of you went to Sunday school as a child (I'm going to use the Christian context in this discussion) and went to church with your parents in adolescence, but left religion behind as you were socialized by college. By *socialized*, I don't mean that you studied theology under professors who convinced you that Thomas Aquinas was wrong. You didn't study theology at all. None of the professors you admired were religious. When the topic of religion came up, they treated it dismissively or as a subject of humor. You went along with the zeitgeist.

I am describing my own religious life from the time I went to Harvard until my late forties. At that point my wife, prompted by the birth of our first child, had found a religious tradition in which she was comfortable, Quakerism, and had been attending Quaker meetings for several years. By the early 1990s, I was occasionally keeping her company. That was twenty years ago. Since then, my wife has become an increasingly serious Quaker. I still describe myself as an agnostic, but I'm shakier in my nonbelief. Watching her has taught me some things that I pass along to you with the recommendation that you don't wait as long as I did to get serious.

Taking religion seriously means homework. If you're waiting for a road-to-Damascus experience, you're kidding yourself. Taking one of the great religions seriously, getting inside its rich body of thought, doesn't happen by sitting on beaches, watching sunsets, and waiting for enlightenment. It can easily require as much intellectual effort as a law degree. Even dabbling at the edges has demonstrated the truth of that statement to me for Judaism, Buddhism, and Taoism. I assume it's true of Islam and Hinduism as well. In the case of Christianity, with which I'm most familiar, the church has produced profound religious thinkers for two thousand years. You don't have to go back to Thomas Aquinas (though that wouldn't be a bad idea). Just the last century has produced excellent and accessible work. But whomever you read, Christianity considered seriously bears little resemblance to your Sunday school lessons. You've got to grapple with the real thing.

A good way to jar yourself out of unreflective atheism is to read about contemporary science. The progress of science from Copernicus until the end of the nineteenth century delivered one body blow after another to simplistic religious beliefs. First, it turned out that the earth wasn't the center of the universe. It wasn't even the center of our solar system. Then the Newtonian laws of physics set up the image of a clockwork universe that didn't need a God to make it run. Then Reason with a capital *R* was enthroned during the Enlightenment, in direct conflict with the intrinsic nature of religious faith. Then Darwin destroyed the creation myth. Then Freud destroyed our confidence that we were autonomous beings and told us that faith was nothing more than wish fulfillment.

But in the late nineteenth century quantum physics was born, and with it began the story of an underlying physical reality that was not only stranger than we knew but stranger than we could have imagined. That story is still unfolding—dark matter is just one of the mysteries left to be solved, and entanglement is now accepted as proven with no one having the slightest idea how it works. The twentieth century also revolutionized our understanding of the universe and its origins. Suppose at the beginning of the twentieth century an astronomer had announced that the universe began with a big bang in which space, time, and the raw materials for the stars and planets suddenly emerged out of a timeless, spaceless singularity. He would have been laughed off the platform, because obviously what he had done was drape scientific language over the creation story in Genesis—"And God said, 'Let there be light,' and there was light." But it turns out that my imaginary silly astronomer was right. That's how the universe really did get started.

After the Big Bang became accepted science, astrophysics began to calculate the infinitesimally small probability that any Big Bang would produce a universe capable of sustaining life—so infinitesimally small that the theory of multiple universes has become the necessary default explanation. Unless you posit multiple universes (and a whole lot of them too), either we are a one-in-a-billion chance or some power created the universe explicitly so that it would produce life. It sounds weird, I know, but check it out. *Just Six Numbers* by

Martin Rees, Britain's Astronomer Royal, who is not himself religious, is a good starting point.

The more you are around people who are seriously religious, the harder it is to think there's nothing to it. I say this mostly out of my wife's testimony, because she has been around some impressive examples, but to some extent from my own experience. You will encounter people whose intelligence, judgment, and critical faculties are as impressive as those of your smartest atheist friends—and who also possess a disquietingly serene confidence in an underlying reality behind the many religious dogmas. They have learned to reconcile faith and reason, yes, but beyond that, they persuasively convey that there are ways of knowing that transcend intellectual understanding. They exhibit in their own personae a kind of wisdom that goes beyond just having intelligence and good judgment.

If any of these propositions has intrigued you enough to start taking religion seriously, here's a short reading list for Christianity (if you're Jewish, a sympathetic rabbi can get you started). My favorite entry point is *Mere Christianity* by C. S. Lewis. The book is a compilation of radio lectures on the BBC during World War II. It is effortless to read, is charming, radiates intelligence, and will get you thinking. Thomas Merton's *The Seven Storey Mountain* is a classic account of a spiritual journey from youth to maturity. If you want an example of a book that will show you how much more there is to the Gospels than you realized, read *The Wisdom Jesus* by Cynthia Bourgeault.

None of this material is boring. On the contrary, it's riveting. I could legitimately say, "Have fun," but there's more to it than that.

32. Take the clichés about marriage seriously.

As with the clichés about fame and fortune, the clichés about marriage have become clichés for a reason: They're mostly true. I have nothing original to add. But let me go over the basics anyway, in case it's helpful for someone other than your parents to tell you these things.

Marry someone with similar tastes and preferences. Which tastes and preferences? The ones that will affect life almost every day. It's okay if you like the ballet and your spouse doesn't. Reasonable people can accommodate each other on such differences. But if you dislike each other's friends, or don't get each other's sense of humor, or—especially—if you have different ethical impulses, break it off and find someone else.

Personal habits that you find objectionable in each other might be deal-breakers. Jacques Barzun identified the top three as punctuality, orderliness, and thriftiness. It doesn't make any difference which point of the spectrum you're on, he observed—"Some couples are very happy living always in debt, always being late, and finding leftover pizza under a sofa cushion." You just have to be at the same point on the spectrum. Intractable differences on any one of the three will, over time, become a fingernail dragged across the blackboard of a marriage.

What you see is what you're going to get. If something about your prospective spouse bothers you, but you think that you can change your beloved after you're married, you're wrong. Be prepared to live with whatever bothers you or forget it. Your spouse will undoubtedly change during a long marriage, but not in ways you can predict or control.

It is absolutely crucial that you really, really like your spouse. You hear it all the time from people who are in great marriages: "I'm married to my best friend." They are being literal. They enjoy the day-to-day company of their spouses more than they enjoy the company of anyone else, they can talk to their spouses more openly than they can talk to anyone else, and they can be quietly companionable with their spouses as with no one else. Occasionally this kind of compatibility can develop after marriage, but it's more common to be apparent beforehand. People often lament how hard it is to know whether one is truly in love. That's true. But it's not hard to know how much you *like* someone. Focus on that question even more than you focus on whether you're in love. Here are two things to worry about as you do so:

Do you sometimes pick at each other's sore spots? You have fun together, the sex is great, but one of you is controlling, or nags the other, or won't let a difference of opinion go. Some people have more tolerance of interpersonal conflict than I do, and I'm told that some people actually enjoy the occasional nonviolent fight, so maybe my advice is not generalizable to everyone, but I believe that two people who love each other should be careful to avoid saying anything that will inflict hurt. Occasionally there will be an overwhelmingly compelling reason why the hurtful thing must be said. But if your prospective spouse says hurtful things heedlessly, or seems to take any pleasure whatsoever in causing hurt, break it off.

Is it a grand passion? You know it's a grand passion if you can think of nothing but your beloved, your mood swings wildly depending on your beloved's approval or disapproval, you are experiencing the highest highs and the lowest lows you have ever known, you find yourself behaving like an adolescent long after adolescence has passed—in short, you are obsessed and more than a little crazy. Not to worry. Everyone should experience at least one grand passion. Just don't act on it while the storm is raging. Occasionally, as the grand passion subsides, the two people find that they also like each other, and they can go on to make a great marriage. Very occasionally.

A good marriage is the best thing that can ever happen to you. Above all else, realize that this cliché is true. The downside risks of marrying—and they are real—are nothing compared to what you will gain from a good one.

33. Be open to a startup marriage instead of a merger marriage.

People grow up expecting to get married within a certain age range. When I was in college in the early 1960s, the prime marriage years for someone of my background (middle class, college educated) were from graduation to the midtwenties, with late twenties a little strange for men and definitely strange for women. You are coming of age at a time when the thirties are normal, the midtwenties are a little strange, and the early twenties are definitely strange.

I think this cultural shift toward later marriage has been a good thing. A lot of twenty-two-year-olds are saved from bad marriages because they go into relationships at that age assuming that marriage is still out of the question. But should you assume that marriage is still out of the question when you're twenty-five? Twenty-seven? I'm not suggesting that you decide ahead of time that you will get married in your twenties. You've got to wait until the right person comes along. I'm just pointing out that you shouldn't *exclude* the possibility of getting married before thirty. If you get married in your thirties, your marriage is more likely to be a merger. If you get married in your twenties, it is more likely to be a startup. You need to think about the differences between these two kinds of marriages.

If you want to know what a merger marriage is, look at the wedding page of the Sunday edition of the *New York Times.* Here's the kind of thing you're going to see: Thirty-six-year-old Stanford grad and Harvard MBA marries thirty-two-year-old Middlebury grad with a Yale law degree. He's working at a management consulting firm; she's on the partner track at a big law firm. Combined income of the newlyweds is probably already north of $400,000 and will hit seven figures within a few years.

Not all merger marriages are that glittering, of course, but they usually consist of two people who are already established in their careers. Lots of things may be said in favor of a merger marriage. A bride and groom who are both in their thirties are more mature than those in their twenties. Identities are well formed, meaning less risk that one spouse will outgrow the other. Both partners have had many years of single life after college, meaning less risk that one or both partners will feel impelled to make up for their lost youth ten years into the marriage. The high combined income means that the first years of marriage don't have to be spent in a cramped apartment in a dodgy part of town.

But let me put in a word for startup marriages. By startup marriages, I mean that the partners' success is not yet assured. The groom with his new architecture degree is still designing stairwells and the bride is starting her third year of medical school. Their income doesn't leave them quite below the poverty line, but they have to watch every penny.

What are the advantages of a startup marriage? For one thing, you will both have memories of your life together when it was all still up in the air. I'm willing to bet that Bill Gates's fondest memories are of the years when Microsoft went from being a couple of college dropouts in makeshift offices to a player in the new world of information technology, not of the year in which he became the richest man in the world. The same applies to startup marriages. You'll have fun remembering the years when you went from being scared newcomers to the point at which you realized you were going to make it.

Even more important, you and your spouse will

have made your way together. Whatever happens, you will have shared the experience. If the fledgling architect ends up designing landmark skyscrapers and the medical student becomes an esteemed surgeon, both of those successes will have been shared successes. And you will each know that you wouldn't have become the person you are without the other.

I'm not dissing merger marriages. The upsides of merger marriages are worth considering, and many merger marriages are extremely happy ones. But perhaps a certain kind of symbiosis, where two people become more than the sum of the individuals, is more common in startups.

34. Watch *Groundhog Day* repeatedly.

Most of what I have said about human happiness comes directly from Aristotle, so I suppose I should tell you to read his *Nicomachean Ethics* carefully and ponder it in your heart. But let's be realistic: You won't do it. For that matter, it probably wouldn't help if you did. I read the *Nicomachean Ethics* when I was an undergraduate and it didn't register. I found Aristotle's prose archaic and boring—something I had to endure to prepare for the final exam. It wasn't until I was in my forties and had to summarize Aristotle's view of happiness for a book I was writing that I realized how profoundly right he was.

As I come to the end of my advice and send you off into the world, I have an alternative way for you to stay on the straight and narrow: periodically watch *Groundhog Day*. It was made long ago, in 1993, but it's still smart and funny, the chemistry between the stars (Bill Murray and Andie MacDowell) is terrific, and it has a happy ending. *Groundhog Day* is also a profound moral fable that deals with the most fundamental issues of virtue and happiness.

An egocentric TV weatherman played by Bill Murray is sent to Punxsutawney, Pennsylvania, to cover Groundhog Day. He hates the assignment, disdains the town and its people, and can't wait to get back to Pittsburgh. But a snowstorm strikes, he's stuck in Punxsutawney, and when he wakes up the next morning, it is Groundhog Day again. And again and again and again. Director and cowriter Harold Ramis estimates that the movie has to represent at least thirty or forty years' worth of days. We see only a few dozen of them, ending when Bill Murray's character has discovered the secrets of human happiness. Without the slightest bit of preaching, Ramis shows the bumpy, unplanned evolution of his protagonist from a jerk to a fully realized human being—a person who has learned to experience deep and lasting justified satisfaction with life as a whole even though he has only one day to work with.

Ramis's own understanding of the story he is telling is sophisticated and subtle. That's why you should watch the film more than once. You are sure to pick up subtexts the second time that you didn't get the first time. And you'll see even more when, after giving yourself a rest, you watch it a third time. I've lost count of how many times I've watched *Groundhog Day*, but I've always seen something new.

Why is it a good thing to understand this movie so well? Because it will help you live a good life. Absorbing the deep meaning of the *Nicomachean Ethics* will also help you live a good life, but *Groundhog Day* will do it with a lot less effort.

35. That's it.

Try hard. Be true. Enjoy. Godspeed.

ACKNOWLEDGMENTS

I'm so glad that Karlyn Bowman (my boss), Christy Sadler, and Hilary Waterman decided to start a series of tips on grammar and usage for the AEI intranet. If they hadn't, I would never have thought of going public with my curmudgeonly thoughts. Karlyn was also the first to suggest that I assemble the tips into a book. Thanks go as well to the staff of AEI who gave me encouraging feedback and new ideas for topics as the series unfolded.

My peerless agent, Amanda Urban, saw what was wrong with the draft I sent her and provided the guidance I needed to make the next iteration more useful for the reader and more satisfying for me. Anna and Bennett, my children who are still of an age to be part of the target audience, set me straight on a number of things I'd gotten wrong. At Crown, Derek Reed acted as the skeptical reader in my target audience and Roger

Scholl acted as the wise grown-up editor. They each prompted happy improvements in the text.

Writing the original tips for my AEI audience was so much fun that I got the cockeyed idea that I wouldn't show them to Catherine, my wife and editor of everything I have written since 1982, before I submitted them. The prose would be pure me, my authentic voice. I backed down when I realized that the prose for my unadulterated tips wasn't quite right. My voice isn't authentically me without Catherine's help.